Mary E. Wilkins

Young Lucretia

And other stories

Mary E. Wilkins

Young Lucretia
And other stories

ISBN/EAN: 9783743312999

Manufactured in Europe, USA, Canada, Australia, Japa

Cover: Foto ©ninafisch / pixelio.de

Manufactured and distributed by brebook publishing software (www.brebook.com)

Mary E. Wilkins

Young Lucretia

YOUNG LUCRETIA

AND OTHER STORIES

BY

MARY E. WILKINS

AUTHOR OF "A NEW ENGLAND NUN, AND OTHER STORIES"
"A HUMBLE ROMANCE, AND OTHER STORIES" ETC.

ILLUSTRATED

NEW YORK AND LONDON
HARPER & BROTHERS PUBLISHERS

BOOKS BY

MARY E. WILKINS FREEMAN

THE COPY-CAT AND OTHER STORIES.
  Illustrated. Post 8vo.
BY THE LIGHT OF THE SOUL.
  Illustrated. Post 8vo.
THE DEBTOR. Illustrated. Post 8vo.
EVELINA'S GARDEN. 16mo.
THE FAIR LAVINIA. Illustrated. Post 8vo.
GILES CORY, YEOMAN. Illustrated. 32mo.
THE GIVERS. Illustrated. Post 8vo.
A HUMBLE ROMANCE. Post 8vo.
JANE FIELD. Illustrated. Post 8vo.
JEROME—A POOR MAN. Illustrated. Post 8vo.
THE LOVE OF PARSON LORD. Post 8vo.
MADELON. Post 8vo.
A NEW ENGLAND NUN. Post 8vo.
PEMBROKE. Illustrated. Post 8vo.
THE PORTION OF LABOR. Illustrated. Post 8vo.
THE SHOULDERS OF ATLAS.
  Illustrated. Post 8vo.
SILENCE, ETC. Illustrated. Post 8vo.
SIX TREES. Illustrated. Post 8vo.
UNDERSTUDIES. Illustrated. Post 8vo.
THE WINNING LADY AND OTHERS.
  Illustrated. Post 8vo.
THE YATES PRIDE. Illustrated. 16mo.
YOUNG LUCRETIA. Illustrated. Post 8vo.

HARPER & BROTHERS, NEW YORK

Copyright, 1892, by HARPER & BROTHERS.

PRINTED IN THE UNITED STATES OF AMERICA

CONTENTS

	PAGE
YOUNG LUCRETIA	1
HOW FIDELIA WENT TO THE STORE	20
ANN MARY; HER TWO THANKSGIVINGS	37
ANN LIZY'S PATCHWORK	65
THE LITTLE PERSIAN PRINCESS	85
WHERE THE CHRISTMAS-TREE GREW	105
WHERE SARAH JANE'S DOLL WENT	122
SEVENTOES' GHOST	137
LITTLE MIRANDY, AND HOW SHE EARNED HER SHOES	152
A PARSNIP STEW	175
THE DICKEY BOY	193
A SWEET-GRASS BASKET	216
MEHITABLE LAMB	237

ILLUSTRATIONS

	PAGE
"'LUCRETIA RAYMOND, WHAT *DO* YOU MEAN, PUTTING YOUR DRESS ON THIS WAY?'"	*Frontispiece*
"'WHOSE LITTLE GAL AIR YOU?'"	*Facing p.* 26
MR. LITTLE SELECTS THE THANKSGIVING TURKEY	43
"SARAH JANE SAT DOWN BESIDE THE ROAD AND WEPT"	131
THE VISIT TO CAP'N MOSEBY'S	163
"'EAT 'EM!' ORDERED CAP'N MOSEBY"	171
"THERE, AMONG THE BLOSSOMING BRANCHES, CLUNG THE DICKEY BOY"	211
"SHE WAS A REAL INDIAN PRINCESS"	221

YOUNG LUCRETIA

"Who's that little gal goin' by?" said old Mrs. Emmons.

"That—why, that's young Lucretia, mother," replied her daughter Ann, peering out of the window over her mother's shoulder. There was a fringe of flowering geraniums in the window; the two women had to stretch their heads over them.

"Poor little soul!" old Mrs. Emmons remarked further. "I pity that child."

"I don't see much to pity her for," Ann returned, in a voice high-pitched and sharply sweet; she was the soprano singer in the village choir. "I don't see why she isn't taken care of as well as most children."

"Well, I don't know but she's took care of, but I guess she don't get much coddlin'. Lucretia an' Maria ain't that kind—never was. I heerd the other day they was goin' to have a Christmas-tree down to the school-house. Now I'd be willin' to ventur' consider'ble that child don't have a thing on't."

"Well, if she's kept clean an' whole, an' made to behave, it amounts to a good deal more'n Christmas presents, I suppose." Ann sat down and turned a hem with vigor: she was a dressmaker.

"Well, I s'pose it does, but it kinder seems as if that little gal ought to have somethin'. Do you remember them little rag babies I used to make for you, Ann? I s'pose she'd be terrible tickled with one. Some of that blue thibet would be jest the thing to make it a dress of."

"Now, mother, you ain't goin' to fussing. She won't think anything of it."

"Yes, she would, too. You used to take sights of comfort with 'em." Old Mrs. Emmons, tall and tremulous, rose up and went out of the room.

"She's gone after the linen pieces," thought her daughter Ann. "She is dreadfully silly." Ann began smoothing out some remnants of blue thibet on her lap. She selected one piece that she thought would do for the dress.

Meanwhile young Lucretia went to school. It was quite a cold day, but she was warmly dressed. She wore her aunt Lucretia's red and green plaid shawl, which Aunt Lucretia had worn to meeting when she was herself a little girl, over her aunt Maria's black ladies' cloth coat. The coat was very large and roomy—indeed, it had not been altered at all—but the cloth was thick and good. Young Lucretia wore also her aunt Maria's black alpaca dress, which had been somewhat decreased in size to fit her, and her aunt Lucretia's purple hood with a nubia tied over it. She had mittens, a black quilted petticoat, and her aunt Maria's old drab stockings drawn over her shoes to keep the snow from her ankles. If young Lucretia caught cold, it would not be her aunts' fault. She went along rather clumsily, but quite merrily, holding her tin dinner-pail very steady. Her aunts had charged her not to swing it, and "get the dinner in a mess."

Young Lucretia's face, with very pink cheeks, and smooth lines of red hair over the temples, looked gayly and honestly out of the hood and nubia. Here and there along the road were sprigs of evergreen and ground-pine and hemlock. Lucretia glanced a trifle soberly at them. She was nearly in sight of the school-house when she reached Alma Ford's house, and Alma came out and joined her. Alma was trim and pretty in her fur-bordered winter coat and her scarlet hood.

"Hullo, Lucretia!" said Alma.

"Hullo!" responded Lucretia. Then the two little girls trotted on together: the evergreen sprigs were growing thicker. "Did you go?" asked Lucretia, looking down at them.

"Yes; we went way up to the cross-roads. They wouldn't let you go, would they?"

"No," said Lucretia, smiling broadly.

"I think it was *mean*," said Alma.

"They said they didn't approve of it," said Lucretia, in a serious voice, which seemed like an echo of some one else's.

When they got to the school-house it took her a long time to unroll herself from her many wrappings. When at last she emerged there was not another child there who was dressed quite after her fashion. Seen from behind, she looked like a small, tightly-built old lady. Her little basque, cut after her aunt's own pattern, rigorously whaleboned, with long straight seams, opened in front; she wore a dimity ruffle, a square blue bow to fasten it, and a brown gingham apron. Her sandy hair was parted rigorously in the middle, brought over her temples in two smooth streaky scallops, and braided behind in two tight tails, fastened by a green bow. Young Lucretia was a homely little girl, although her face was always radiantly good-humored. She was a good scholar, too, and could spell and add sums as fast as anybody in the school.

In the entry, where she took off her things, there was a great litter of evergreen and hemlock; in the farthest corner, lopped pitifully over on its side, was a fine hemlock-tree. Lucretia looked at it, and her smiling face grew a little serious.

"That the Christmas-tree out there?" she said to the other girls when she went into the school-room. The teacher had not come, and there was such an uproar and jubilation that she could hardly make herself heard. She had to poke one of the girls two or three times before she could get her question answered.

"What did you say, Lucretia Raymond?" she asked.

"That the Christmas-tree out there?"

"Course 'tis. Say, Lucretia, can't you come this evening and help trim? the boys are a-going to set up the tree, and we're going to trim. Say, can't you come?"

Then the other girls joined in: "Can't you come, Lucretia?—say, can't you?"

Lucretia looked at them all, with her honest smile. "I don't believe I can," said she.

"Won't they let you?—won't your aunts let you?"

"Don't believe they will."

Alma Ford stood back on her heels and threw back her chin. "Well, I don't care," said she. "I think your aunts are *awful mean*—so there!"

Lucretia's face got pinker, and the laugh died out of it. She opened her lips, but before she had a chance to speak, Lois Green, who was one of the older girls, and an authority in the school, added her testimony. "They are two mean, stingy old maids," she proclaimed; "that's what they are."

"They're not neither," said Lucretia, unexpectedly. "You sha'n't say such things about my aunts, Lois Green."

"Oh, you can stick up for 'em if you want to," returned Lois, with cool aggravation. "If you want to be such a little gump, you can, an' nobody'll pity you. You know you won't get a single thing on this Christmas-tree."

"I will, too," cried Lucretia, who was fiery, with all her sweetness.

"You won't."

"You see if I don't, Lois Green."

"You won't."

All through the day it seemed to her, the more she thought of it, that she must go with the others to trim the school-house, and she must have something on the Christmas-tree. A keen sense of shame for her aunts and herself was over her; she felt as if she must keep up the family credit.

"I wish I could go to trim this evening," she said to Alma, as they were going home after school.

"Don't you believe they'll let you?"

"I don't believe they'll 'prove of it," Lucretia answered, with dignity.

"Say, Lucretia, do you s'pose it would make any difference if my mother should go up to your house an' ask your aunts?"

Lucretia gave her a startled look: a vision of her aunt's indignation at such interference shot before her eyes. "Oh, I don't believe it would do a mite of good," said she, fervently. "But I tell you what 'tis, Alma, you might come home with me while I ask."

"I will," said Alma, eagerly. "Just wait a minute till I ask mother if I can."

But it was all useless. Alma's pretty, pleading little face as a supplement to Lucretia's, and her timorous, "Please let Lucretia go," had no effect whatever.

"I don't approve of children being out nights," said Aunt Lucretia, and Aunt Maria supported her. "There's no use talking," said she; "you can't go, Lucretia. Not another word. Take your things off, and sit down and sew your square of patchwork before supper. Almy, you'd better run right home; I guess your mother 'll be wanting you to help her." And Alma went.

"What made you bring that Ford girl in here to ask me?" Aunt Lucretia, who had seen straight through her namesake's artifice, asked of young Lucretia.

"I don't know," stammered Lucretia, over her patchwork.

"You'll never go anywhere any quicker for taking such means as that," said Aunt Lucretia.

"It would serve you right if we didn't let you go to the Christmas-tree," declared Aunt Maria, severely, and young Lucretia quaked. She had had the promise of going to the Christmas-tree for a long time. It would be awful if she should lose that. She sewed very diligently on her patchwork. A square a day was her stent, and she had held up before her the rapture and glory of a whole quilt made all by herself before she was ten years old.

Half an hour after tea she had the square all done. "I've got it done," said she, and she carried it over to her aunt Lucretia that it might be inspected.

Aunt Lucretia put on her spectacles and looked closely at it. "You've sewed it very well," she said, finally, in a tone of severe commendation.

"You can sew well enough if you put your mind to it."

"That's what I've always told her," chimed in Aunt Maria. "There's no sense in her slighting her work so, and taking the kind of stitches she does sometimes. Now, Lucretia, it's time for you to go to bed."

Lucretia went lingeringly across the wide old sitting-room, then across the old wide dining-room, into the kitchen. It was quite a time before she got her candle lighted and came back, and then she stood about hesitatingly.

"What are you waiting for?" Aunt Lucretia asked, sharply. "Take care; you're tipping your candle over; you'll get the grease on the carpet."

"Why don't you mind what you're doing?" said Aunt Maria.

Young Lucretia had scant encouragement to open upon the subject in her mind, but she did. "They're going to have lots of presents on the Christmas-tree," she remarked, tipping her candle again.

"Are you going to hold that candle straight or not?" cried Aunt Lucretia. "Who is going to have lots of presents?"

"All the other girls."

When the aunts got very much in earnest

about anything they spoke with such vehement unison that it had the effect of a duet; it was difficult to tell which was uppermost. "Well, the other girls can have lots of presents; if their folks want to get presents for 'em they can," said they. "There's one thing about it, you won't get anything, and you needn't expect anything. I never approved of this giving presents Christmas, anyway. It's an awful tax an' a foolish piece of business."

Young Lucretia's lips quivered so she could hardly speak. "They'll think it's—so—funny if—I don't have—anything," she said.

"Let 'em think it's funny if they want to. You take your candle an' go to bed, an' don't say any more about it. Mind you hold that candle straight."

Young Lucretia tried to hold the candle straight as she went up-stairs, but it was hard work, her eyes were so misty with tears. Her little face was all puckered up with her silent crying as she trudged wearily up the stairs. It was a long time before she got to sleep that night. She cried first, then she meditated. Young Lucretia was too small and innocent to be artful, but she had a keen imagination, and was fertile of resources in emergencies. In the midst of her grief and disappointment she devolved a plan for keeping up the family honor, hers and her aunts', before the eyes of the school.

The next day everything favored the plan. School did not keep; in the afternoon both the aunts went to the sewing society. They had been gone about an hour when young Lucretia trudged down the road with her arms full of parcels. She stole so quietly and softly into the school-house, where they were arranging the tree, that no one thought about it. She laid the parcels on a settee with some others, and stole out and flew home.

The festivities at the school-house began at seven o'clock. There were to be some exercises, some recitations and singing, then the distribution of the presents. Directly after tea young Lucretia went up to her own little chamber to get ready. She came down in a surprisingly short time all dressed.

"Are you all ready?" said Aunt Lucretia.

"Yes, ma'am," replied young Lucretia. She had her hand on the door-latch.

"I don't believe you are half dressed," said Aunt Maria. "Did you get your bow on straight?"

"Yes, ma'am."

"I think she'd better take her things off, an' let us be sure," said Aunt Lucretia. "I'm not goin' to have her down there with her clothes on any which way, an' everybody making remarks. Take your sacque off, Lucretia."

"Oh, I got the bow on straight; it's real straight, it is, *honest*," pleaded young Lucretia, piteously. She clutched the plaid shawl tightly together, but it was of no use—off the things had to come. And young Lucretia had put on the prim whaleboned basque of her best dress wrong side before; she had buttoned it in the back. There she stood, very much askew and uncomfortable about the shoulder seams and sleeves, and hung her head before her aunts.

"Lucretia Raymond, what *do* you mean, putting your dress on this way?"

"All—the other—girls—wear—theirs buttoned in—the back."

"All the other girls! Well, you're not going to have yours buttoned in the back, and wear holes through that nice ladies' cloth coat every time you lean back against a chair. I should think you were crazy. I've a good mind not to let you go out at all. Stand round here!"

Young Lucretia's basque was sharply unbuttoned, she was jerked out of it, and it was turned around and fastened as it was meant to be. When she was finally started, with her aunts' parting admonition echoing after her, she felt sad and doubtful, but soon her merry disposition asserted itself.

There was no jollier and more radiant little soul than she all through the opening exercises. She listened to the speaking and the singing with the greatest appreciation and delight. She sat up perfectly straight in her prim and stiff basque; she folded her small red hands before her; her two tight braids inclined stiffly towards her ears, and her face was all aglow with smiles.

When the distribution of presents began her name was among the first called. She arose with alacrity, and went with a gay little prance down the aisle. She took the parcel that the teacher handed to her; she commenced her journey back, when she suddenly encountered the eyes of her aunt Lucretia and her aunt Maria. Then her terror and remorse began. She had never dreamed of such a thing as her aunts coming—indeed, they had not themselves. A neighbor had come in and persuaded them, and they had taken a sudden start against their resolutions and their principles.

Young Lucretia's name was called again and again. Every time she slunk more reluctantly and fearfully down to the tree; she knew that her aunts' eyes were surveying her with more and more amazement.

After the presents were all distributed she sat perfectly still with hers around her. They lay on her desk, and the last one was in her lap. She had not taken off a single wrapping. They were done up neatly in brown paper, and Lucretia's name was written on them.

Lucretia sat there. The other girls were in a hubbub of delight all around her, comparing their presents, but she sat perfectly still and watched her aunts coming. They came slowly; they stopped to speak to the teacher. Aunt Lucretia reached young Lucretia first.

"What have you got there?" she asked. She did not look cross, but a good deal surprised. Young Lucretia just gazed miserably up at her. "Why don't you undo them?" asked Aunt Lucretia. Young Lucretia shook her head helplessly. "Why, what makes you act so, child?" cried Aunt Lucretia, getting alarmed. Then Aunt Maria came up, and there was quite a little group around young Lucretia. She began to cry. "What on earth ails the child?" said Aunt Lucretia. She caught up one of the parcels and opened it; it was a book bound in red and gold. She held it close to her eyes; she turned it this way and that; she examined the fly-leaf. "Why," said she, "it's the old gift-book Aunt

Susan gave me when I was eighteen years old! What in the world!"

Aunt Maria had undone another. "This is the *Floral Album*," she said, tremulously; "we always keep it in the north parlor on the table. Here's my name in it. I don't see—"

Aunt Lucretia speechlessly unmuffled a clove apple and a nautilus shell that had graced the parlor shelf; then a little daintily dressed rag doll with cheeks stained pink with cranberry juice appeared. When young Lucretia spied this last she made a little grab at it.

"Oh," she sobbed, "somebody did hang this on for me! They did—they did! It's mine!"

It never seemed to young Lucretia that she walked going home that night; she had a feeling that only her tiptoes occasionally brushed the earth; she went on rapidly, with a tall aunt on either side. Not much was said. Once in a lonely place in the road there was a volley of severe questions from her aunts, and young Lucretia burst out in a desperate wail. "Oh!" she cried, "I was going to put 'em right back again, I was! I've not hurt 'em any. I was real careful. I didn't s'pose you'd know it. Oh, they said you were cross an' stingy, an' wouldn't hang me anything on the tree, an' I didn't want 'em to think you were. I wanted to make 'em think I had things, I did."

"What made you think of such a thing?"

"I don't know."

"I shouldn't think you would know. I never heard of such doings in my life!"

After they got home not much was said to young Lucretia; the aunts were still too much bewildered for many words. Lucretia was bidden to light her candle and go to bed, and then came a new grief, which was the last drop in the bucket for her. They confiscated her rag doll, and put it away in the parlor with the clove apple, the nautilus shell, and the gift-book. Then the little girl's heart failed her, remorse for she hardly knew what, terror, and the loss of the sole comfort that had come to her on this pitiful Christmas Eve were too much.

"Oh," she wailed, "my rag baby! my rag baby! I—want my—rag baby. Oh! oh! oh! I want her, I want her."

Scolding had no effect. Young Lucretia sobbed out her complaint all the way up-stairs, and her aunts could distinguish the pitiful little wail of my "rag baby, I want my rag baby," after she was in her chamber.

The two women looked at each other. They had sat uneasily down by the sitting-room fire.

"I must say that I think you're rather hard on her, Lucretia," said Maria, finally.

"I don't know as I've been any harder on her than you have," returned Lucretia. "I shouldn't have said to take away that rag baby if I'd said just what I thought."

"I think you'd better take it up to her, then, and stop that crying," said Maria.

Lucretia hastened into the north parlor without another word. She carried the rag baby upstairs to young Lucretia; then she came down to the pantry and got a seed-cake for her. "I thought the child had better have a little bite of something; she didn't eat scarcely a mite of supper," she explained to Maria. She had given young Lucretia's head a hard pat when she bestowed the seed-cake, and bade her eat it and go right to sleep. The little girl hugged her rag baby and ate her cooky in bliss.

The aunts sat a while longer by the sitting-room fire. Just before they left it for the night Lucretia looked hesitatingly at Maria, and said,

"I s'pose you have noticed that wax doll down to White's store, 'ain't you?"

"That big wax one with the pink dress?" asked Maria, faintly and consciously.

"Yes. There was a doll's bedstead there, too. I don't know as you noticed."

"Yes, I think I did, now you speak of it. I noticed it the day I went in for the calico. There was a doll baby's carriage there, too."

The aunts looked at each other. "I s'pose it would be dreadful foolish," said Lucretia.

"She'd be 'most too tickled to live," remarked Maria.

"Well, we can't buy 'em to-night anyway," said Lucretia. "I must light the candles an' lock up."

The next day was Christmas. It was about three o'clock in the afternoon when old Mrs. Emmons went up the road to the Raymond house. She had a little parcel. When she came into the sitting-room there was young Lucretia in a corner, so that the room should not get in a mess, with her wealth around her. She looked forth, a radiant little mother of dolls, from the midst of her pretty miniature house-keeping.

"My sakes!" cried old Mrs. Emmons, "isn't that complete? She's got a big wax doll, an' a bedstead, an' a baby-carriage, an' a table an' bureau. I declare! Well, I don't know what I should have thought when I was a little gal. An' I've brought some pieces for you to make some more dresses for the rag baby, if you want to."

Young Lucretia's eyes shone.

"You were real kind to think of it," said Aunt Lucretia; "an' she'll take real comfort making the dresses. I'm real glad you came in, Mis' Emmons. I've been going down to see you for a long time. I want to see Ann, too; I thought I'd see if she hadn't got a pattern of a dress that buttons up in the back for Lucretia."

Young Lucretia's eyes shone more than ever, and she smiled out of her corner like a little star.

HOW FIDELIA WENT TO THE STORE

"I don't know what we're goin' to do," said Aunt Maria Crooker. She sat in a large armchair, and held in her lap a bowl of sugar and butter that she was creaming. Aunt Maria filled up the chair from arm to arm, for she was very portly; she had a large, rosy, handsome face, and she creamed with such energy that she panted for breath.

"Well, I don't know, either," rejoined her sister, Mrs. Lennox. "I can't go to the store with my lame foot, that's certain."

"Well, I know *I* can't," said Aunt Maria, with additional emphasis. "I haven't walked two mile for ten year, an' I don't believe I could get to that store and back to save my life."

"I don't believe you could, either. I don't know what is goin' to be done. We can't make the cake without raisins, anyhow. It's the queerest thing how father happened to forget them.

Now here he is gone over to East Dighton after the new cow, and Cynthy gone to Keene to buy her bonnet, an' me with a scalt foot, an' you not able to walk, an' not one raisin in the house to put into that weddin'-cake."

Mrs. Lennox stated the case in full, with a despairing eloquence, and Aunt Maria sighed and wrinkled her forehead.

"If there were only any neighbors you could borrow from," she observed.

"Well, there ain't any neighbors 'twixt here and the store except the Allens and the Simmonses, and the Allens are so tight they never put raisins into their Thanksgivin' pies. Mis' Allen told me they didn't. She said she thought most folks made their pies too rich, an' her folks liked them just as well without raisins. An' as for the Simmonses, I don't believe they see a raisin from one year's end to the other. They're lucky if they can get enough common things to eat for all those children. I don't know what's goin' to be done. Here's the dress-maker comin' to-morrow, an' Cynthy goin' to be married in two weeks, and the cake ought to be made to-day if it's ever goin' to be."

"Yes, it had," assented Aunt Maria. "We've put it off full long enough, anyway. Weddin'-cake ain't near so good unless it stands a little while."

"I know it."

Just then there was a shrill, prolonged squeak. It came from the yard. The doors and windows were open; it was a very warm day.

"What's that?" cried Aunt Maria.

"Oh, it's nothin' but Fidelia's little wagon. She's draggin' it round the yard."

The two women looked at each other; it was as if a simultaneous idea had come suddenly to them.

Aunt Maria gave expression to it first. "Fidelia couldn't go, could she?"

"Maria Crooker, that little thing! She ain't six years old, an' she's never been anywhere alone. Do you s'pose I'm goin' to send her a mile to that store?" Mrs. Lennox's tone was full of vehement indignation, but her eyes still met Aunt Maria's with that doubtful and reflective expression.

"I don't see a mite of harm in it," Aunt Maria maintained, sturdily. She set her bowl of sugar and butter on the table, and leaned forward with a hand on each aproned knee. "I know Fidelia ain't but five year old, but she's brighter than some children of seven. It's just a straight road to the store, an' she can't get lost, to save her life. And she knows where 'tis. You took her down to Mis' Rose's three or four weeks ago, didn't you?"

"Yes; that day father went down for grain. I s'pose she would remember."

"Of course she'd remember. I don't see one thing, as far as I'm concerned, to hinder that child's goin' down to the store an' bringin' home some raisins. I used to go on errands before I was as old as she is. Folks didn't fuss over their children so much in my day."

"Well," said Mrs. Lennox, finally, with a great sigh, "I don't know but I may as well send her."

Mrs. Lennox was much smaller than her sister, and she had a rather sickly but pleasant face. She had to push a chair before her as she walked, for she had scalded her foot quite badly the week before, and it was now all swathed in bandages. It had been a very unfortunate accident in more ways than one, for Cynthia, her elder daughter, was going to be married soon, and the family were busily engaged in the wedding preparations. It was very hard for poor Mrs. Lennox to have to limp about with one knee in a chair, while she made wedding-cake and arranged for the bridal festivities, but she made the best of it.

Now she pushed over to the door, and called, "Fidelia! Fidelia!"

Directly the squeak increased to an agonizing degree, the rattle of small wheels accompanied it, and Fidelia came trudging around the corner of the house. She was a chubby little girl, and her blue tier seemed rather tight for her. She had a round, rosy face, and innocent and honest black eyes. She wore a small Shaker bonnet with a green cape, and she stubbed her toes into the grass every step she took.

"Don't stub your toes so," said her mother, admonishingly. "You'll wear your shoes all out."

Fidelia immediately advanced with soft pats like a kitten. When she got into the kitchen her mother took off her Shaker bonnet and looked at her critically. "You'll have to have your hair brushed," said she. "Fidelia, do you remember how you went with mother down to Mis' Rose's three or four weeks ago?"

Fidelia nodded and winked.

"There was a big pussy cat there, do you remember? and Mis' Rose gave you a cooky."

Fidelia's affirmative wink seemed to give out sparkles.

"Well, you remember how we went to the *side* door and knocked—the door with some roses over the top of it—and Mis' Rose came—the *side* door?"

Fidelia, intensely attentive, standing before her mother and Aunt Maria, remembered about the side door.

"Well, you remember how there was a piazza

across the front of the house, don't you? Father hitched the horse to a post there. Well, there's another door there opening on the piazza, don't you remember—a door with panes of glass in it like a window?"

Fidelia remembered.

"Well, now, Fidelia, do you suppose you can go down to the store and buy some raisins for mother to put in sister Cynthy's weddin'-cake, all yourself?"

"An' be a real smart little girl," put in Aunt Maria.

Fidelia gave one ecstatic roll of her black eyes at them, then she broke into a shout, "Lemme go! lemme go!" She oscillated on her small stubbed toes like a bird preparing to fly, and she tugged energetically at her mother's apron.

"I'll give you a penny, an' you can buy you a nice stick of red-and-white twisted candy," added her mother.

Fidelia actually made a little dash for the door then, but her mother caught her. "Stop!" she said, in an admonitory voice which was quieting to Fidelia, and made her realize that the red-and-white candy was still in the future. "Now you just wait a minute, an' not be in such a pucker. You ain't goin' this way, with your apron just as dirty as poison, and your hair all in a snarl.

You've got to have on your clean apron, and have your hair brushed and your face washed."

So Fidelia climbed obediently into her high chair, and sat with her eyes screwed up and her fists clinched, while her mother polished her face faithfully with a wet, soapy end of a towel, and combed the snarls out of her hair. When it was all done, her cheeks being very red and shiny, and her hair very damp and smooth, when she was arrayed in her clean starched white tier, and had her Shaker tied on with an emphatic square bow, she stood in the door and drank in the parting instructions. Her eyes were wide and intent, and her mouth drooped soberly at the corners. The importance of the occasion had begun to impress her. She held a penny tight in her hand; the raisins were to be charged, it not being judged advisable to trust Fidelia with so much money.

"I don't believe that little thing can carry three pounds of raisins," Mrs. Lennox said to Aunt Maria. She was becoming more and more uneasy about Fidelia's going.

"Let her take her little wagon an' drag 'em; that'll be just the thing," said Aunt Maria, complacently.

So Fidelia started down the road, trundling behind her the little squeaking cart. It was a

"'WHOSE LITTLE GAL AIR YOU?'"

warm July day, and it was very dusty. Directly Fidelia started she forgot her mother's injunctions about stubbing her toes; she disappeared in a small cloud of dust, for she walked in the middle of the road, and flirted it up with great delight.

In the course of the mile Fidelia met one team. It was an old rocking chaise and a white horse, and an old farmer was driving. He drove slower when he came alongside of Fidelia. When he had fairly passed her he stopped entirely, twisted about in his seat, and raised his voice.

"Whose little gal air you?" he asked.

Fidelia was a little frightened. Instead of giving her father's name, she gave her own with shy precision—"Fidelia Ames Lennox," she said, retiring into her Shaker bonnet.

"You ain't runnin' away, be you?"

Fidelia's pride was touched. "I'm going to the store for my mother," she announced, in quite a shrill tone. Then she took to her heels, and the little wagon trundled after, with a wilder squeak than ever.

Fidelia kept saying over to herself, "Three pounds of your best raisins, and Mr. Lennox will come in and pay you." Her mother and Aunt Maria wished after she had gone that they had written it out on a piece of paper; they had not thought of that. But Aunt Maria said she knew that such a bright child as Fidelia would remember three pounds of raisins when she had been told over and over, and charged not to come home without them.

Fidelia had started about ten o'clock in the morning, and her mother and Aunt Maria had agreed that they would not worry if she should not return until one o'clock in the afternoon. That would allow more than an hour for the mile walk each way, and give plenty of time for a rest between; for Fidelia had been instructed to go into the store and sit down on a stool and rest a while before starting upon her return trip. "Likely as not Mis' Rose will give her a cooky or something," Aunt Maria had whispered to Mrs. Lennox.

So when noon came the two women pictured Fidelia sitting perched upon a stool in the store, being fed with candy and cookies, and made much of, or even eating dinner with the Rose family. "Mis' Rose made so much of her when you took her there before that I shouldn't wonder a mite if she'd kept her to dinner," said Aunt Maria. She promulgated this theory the more strenuously when one o'clock came and Fidelia had not appeared. "Of course that's what 'tis," she kept repeating. "It would take 'em a good hour to eat dinner. I shouldn't be a bit surprised if she didn't get here before two o'clock. I think you're dreadful silly to worry, Jane."

For poor Mrs. Lennox was pushing her chair every few minutes over to the door, where she would stand, her face all one anxious frown, straining her eyes for a glimpse of the small figure trudging up the road. She had made the blueberry dumpling that Fidelia loved for dinner, and it was keeping warm on the back of the stove. Neither she nor Aunt Maria had eaten a mouthful.

When two o'clock came Mrs. Lennox broke down entirely. "Oh dear!" she wailed; "oh dear! I ought to have known better than to let her go."

Aunt Maria was now pacing heavily between her chair and the door, but she still maintained a brave front. "For goodness' sake, Jane, don't give up so," said she. "I don't see anything to worry about, for my part; they're keepin' her."

At half-past two Mrs. Lennox stood up with a determined air. "I ain't goin' to wait here another minute," said she. "I'm goin' to find her. I don't know but she's fell into the brook, or got run over." Mrs. Lennox's face was all drawn with anxiety.

"I'd like to know how you're goin'," said Aunt Maria.

"I guess I can push this chair along the road just as well as in a room."

"Pretty-lookin' sight you'd be goin' a mile with one knee in a wooden chair."

"I guess I don't care much how I look if I only find—her." Mrs. Lennox's voice broke into a wail.

"You just sit down and keep calm," said Aunt Maria. "If anybody's goin', I am."

"Oh, you can't."

"Yes, I can, too. I ain't quite so far gone that I can't walk a mile. You ain't goin' a step on that scalt foot an' get laid up, with that weddin' comin' off, not if I know it. I'm just goin' to slip on my gaiter-shoes an' my sun-bonnet, an' take the big green umbrella to keep the sun off."

When Aunt Maria was equipped and started, Mrs. Lennox watched her progress down the road with frantic impatience. It seemed to her that she could have gone faster with her chair. Truth was, that poor Aunt Maria, plodding heavily along in her gaiter-shoes, holding the green umbrella over her flaming face, made but slow and painful progress, and it was well that Mr. Lennox and Cynthia Lennox came home two hours before they were expected. It was three o'clock when Mr. Lennox came driving into the yard in the open buggy. Cynthia, erect and blooming, with her big bandbox in her lap, sat beside him, and the new Jersey cow, fastened by a rope to the tail of the buggy, came on behind with melancholy moos. Cynthia had bought her wedding-bonnet sooner than she had expected, so she had come home on the three o'clock train instead of the five; and her father had bought the cow sooner than he had expected, and had come to the railroad crossing just about the time that Cynthia's train arrived. So he had stopped and taken in her and her bandbox, and they had all ridden home together.

Mrs. Lennox stood in the kitchen door when they drove in.

"Oh, mother," Cynthia cried out, "I've had splendid luck! I've got the handsomest bonnet!"

"I guess you won't care much about bonnets," answered her mother; "*Fidelia's lost*." She spoke quite slowly and calmly, then she began to weep wildly and lament. It was quite a time before she could make the case plain to them, and Cynthia and her bandbox, and Mr. Lennox and the horse and buggy and cow, all remained before her in a petrified halt.

As soon as Mr. Lennox fairly understood, he sprang out of the buggy, untied the cow, led her into the barn, turned the team around, with a sharp grate of the wheels, jumped in again, and gathered up the reins. Cynthia, her rosy cheeks quite pale, still sat in her place, and the tears splashed on her new bandbox cover. Mrs. Lennox had set her chair outside the door, and followed it, with a painful effort. "Stop, father!" she cried; "I'm goin' too!"

"Oh, mother, you can't!" said Mr. Lennox and Cynthia, together.

"I'm goin'. You needn't say a word. Father, you get out an' help me in."

Mr. Lennox got out and lifted, while Cynthia pulled. Mrs. Lennox's injured foot suffered, but she set her mouth hard, and said nothing. They started at a good pace, three on a seat, with Mr. Lennox in the middle, driving.

They had got about half-way to the store when they overtook Aunt Maria. Aunt Maria, with the green umbrella overhead, was proceeding steadily, with a sideways motion that seemed more effective than the forward one.

"I'll get out, and let her get in," said Cynthia.

"No," said her father; "it won't do; it 'ill break the springs. We can't ride three on a seat with Aunt Maria, anyhow, and I've got to drive."

So they passed Aunt Maria.

"Don't go any farther, Aunt Maria," Cynthia called, sobbingly, back to her. "You sit down on the wall and rest."

But Aunt Maria shook her head, she could not speak, and kept on.

It was quarter-past three when they reached the Rose house and the store. The store was in the front of the house, and the Rose family occupied the rear portion. The house stood on a street corner, so a good deal of it was visible, and the whole establishment had a shut-up air; not a single farmer's wagon stood before the store. However, as Mr. Lennox drove up, a woman's head appeared at a window; then a side door opened, and she stood there. She had on a big apron, and her face was flushed as if she had been over the stove; she held a great wooden spoon, too. She began talking to the Lennoxes, but they paid no attention to her—their eyes were riveted upon the store door. There was a speck of white against its dark front, and suddenly it moved. It was Fidelia's white tier.

"Why, there's Fidelia!" gasped Cynthia. She jumped out, not waiting for her father to turn the wheel, and ran to the store door. The bandbox rolled out and the lid came off, and there was her wedding-bonnet in the dust, but she did not mind that. She caught Fidelia. "Oh, you naughty little girl, where have you been all this time?" cried she.

Fidelia's eyes took on a bewildered stare, her mouth puckered more and more. She clung to her sister, and sobbed something that was quite inaudible. It was quite a time before her father and mother and Cynthia and Mrs. Rose, surrounding her with attention, could gather that the import of it all was that she had knocked and knocked and nobody had come to the door.

"*Knocked!*" gasped Mrs. Rose; "why, the poor little lamb! Here Mr. Rose and Sam have been away all day, an' I've been makin' currant-jell' out in the kitchen. An' there's the bell on the counter, that customers always ring when there ain't anybody round. I've been listenin' for *that* all day. It's been so hot, an' everybody hayin', that I don't suppose a soul but her has been near the store since nine o'clock this mornin', and there she's stood an' knocked. I never heard anything like it in my life. See here, Pussy, haven't you been asleep?"

Fidelia shook her head in a sulky and downcast manner, but there was a suspiciously flushed and creasy look about her, and they agreed that it was more than probable that a nap on the store steps had softened and shortened her vigil.

Mrs. Lennox had her up in the wagon on

her lap. She took her Shaker bonnet off, and smoothed her hair and kissed her. "She thought she'd got to knock, I s'pose," said she. "I ought to have told her she didn't have to when she went to a store. Poor little soul! mother won't send her to the store again till she's bigger."

"I knocked an' knocked," wailed Fidelia, piteously.

She looked cross and worn out. Mrs. Rose ran into the house, and brought out a plate of cookies and a mug of milk, and then Fidelia sat in her mother's lap and ate and drank and felt comforted. But after the raisins had been finally purchased, Cynthia's bonnet picked up out of the dust and shaken, the little squeaking wagon stowed under the seat of the buggy, and the team turned around, Fidelia set up a grievous and injured cry: "My candy! my candy! I 'ain't — got my candy!" And she held up to view the copper cent still clutched in her moist little fist.

"Poor little lamb, she shall have her candy!" cried Mrs. Rose. Fidelia had never seen such a handful of candy as Mrs. Rose brought out from the store. There was a twisted red-and-white stick of peppermint, pink checkerberry, clear barley — a stick of every kind in the glass jars in Mr. Rose's store window. And Mrs. Rose would not take Fidelia's one penny at all; she bade her keep it until she came to the store again.

Aunt Maria was almost up to the store when they left it, and it was decided that she should remain and make a call upon Mrs. Rose while Mr. Lennox carried the others home, then he would return for her. Aunt Maria folded her green umbrella and sank down on the door-step, and Mrs. Rose brought her a palm-leaf fan and a glass of ginger water. "I 'ain't walked a mile before for ten year," gasped Aunt Maria; "but I'm so thankful that child's safe that I can't think of anything else." There were tears in her eyes as she watched the wagon-load disappearing under the green branches of the elm-trees. And Fidelia, in her mother's lap, rode along and sucked a stick of barley candy in silent bliss. Griefs in childhood soon turn to memories; straightway, as she sucked her barley candy, Fidelia's long and painful vigil at the store door became a thing of the past.

ANN MARY

HER TWO THANKSGIVINGS

"Grandma."

"What is it, child?"

"You goin' to put that cup-cake into the pan to bake it now, grandma?"

"Yes; I guess so. It's beat 'bout enough."

"You ain't put in a mite of nutmeg, grandma."

The grandmother turned around to Ann Mary. "Don't you be quite so anxious," said she, with sarcastic emphasis. "I allers put the nutmeg in cup-cake the very last thing. I ruther guess I shouldn't have put this cake into the oven without nutmeg!"

The old woman beat fiercely on the cake. She used her hand instead of a spoon, and she held the yellow mixing-bowl poised on her hip under her arm. She was stout and rosy-faced. She had crinkly white hair, and she always wore a string of gold beads around her creasy neck. She never took off the gold beads except to put them under her pillow at night, she was so afraid of their being stolen. Old Mrs. Little had always been nervous about thieves, although none had ever troubled her.

"You may go into the pantry, an' bring out the nutmeg now, Ann Mary" said she presently, with dignity.

Ann Mary soberly slipped down from her chair and went. She realized that she had made a mistake. It was quite an understood thing for Ann Mary to have an eye upon her grandmother while she was cooking, to be sure that she put in everything that she should, and nothing that she should not, for the old woman was absent-minded. But it had to be managed with great delicacy, and the corrections had to be quite irrefutable, or Ann Mary was reprimanded for her pains.

When Ann Mary had deposited the nutmeg-box and the grater at her grandmother's elbow, she took up her station again. She sat at a corner of the table in one of the high kitchen-chairs. Her feet could not touch the floor, and they dangled uneasily in their stout leather shoes, but she never rested them on the chair round, nor even swung them by way of solace. Ann Mary's grandmother did not like to have her chair rounds all marked up by shoes, and swinging feet disturbed her while she was cooking. Ann Mary sat up, grave and straight. She was a delicate, slender little girl, but she never stooped. She had an odd resemblance to her grandmother; a resemblance more of manner than of feature. She held back her narrow shoulders in the same determined way in which the old woman held her broad ones; she walked as she did, and spoke as she did.

Mrs. Little was very proud of Ann Mary Evans; Ann Mary was her only daughter's child, and had lived with her grandmother ever since she was a baby. The child could not remember either her father or mother, she was so little when they died.

Ann Mary was delicate, so she did not go to the village to the public school. Miss Loretta Adams, a young lady who lived in the neighborhood, gave her lessons. Loretta had graduated in a beautiful white muslin dress at the high-school over in the village, and Ann Mary had a great respect and admiration for her. Loretta had a parlor-organ, and could play on it, and she was going to give Ann Mary lessons after Thanksgiving. Just now there was a vacation. Loretta had gone to Boston to spend two weeks with her cousin.

Ann Mary was all in brown, a brown calico dress and a brown calico, long-sleeved apron; and her brown hair was braided in two tight little tails that were tied with some old brown bonnet-strings of Mrs. Little's, and flared out stiffly behind the ears. Once, when Ann Mary was at her house, Loretta Adams had taken it upon herself to comb out the tight braids and set the hair flowing in a fluffy mass over the shoulders; but when Ann Mary came home her grandmother was properly indignant. She seized her and re-braided the tails with stout and painful jerks. "I ain't goin' to have Loretty Adams meddlin' with your hair," said she, "an' she can jest understand it. If she wants to have her own hair all in a frowzle, an' look like a wild Injun, she can; you sha'n't!"

And Ann Mary, standing before her grandmother with head meekly bent and watery eyes, decided that she would have to tell Loretta that she mustn't touch the braids, if she proposed it again.

That morning, while Mrs. Little was making the pies, and the cake, and the pudding, Ann Mary was sitting idle, for her part of the Thanksgiving cooking was done. She had worked so fast the day before and early that morning that she had the raisins all picked over and seeded, and the apples pared and sliced; and that was about all that her grandmother thought she could do. Ann Mary herself was of a different opinion; she was twelve years old, if she *was* small for her age, and she considered herself quite capable of making pies and cup-cake.

However, it was something to sit there at the table and have that covert sense of superintending her grandmother, and to be reasonably sure that some of the food would have a strange flavor were it not for her vigilance.

Mrs. Little's mince-pies had all been baked the day before; to-day, as she said, she was "making apple and squash." While the apple-pies were in progress, Ann Mary watched her narrowly. Her small folded hands twitched and her little neck seemed to elongate above her apron; but she waited until her grandmother took up an upper crust, and was just about to lay it over a pie. Then she spoke up suddenly. Her voice had a timid yet assertive chirp like a bird's.

"Grandma!"

"Well, what is it, child?"

"You goin' to put that crust on that pie now, grandma?"

Mrs. Little stood uneasily reflective. She eyed the pie sharply. "Yes, I be. Why?" she returned, in a doubtful yet defiant manner.

"You haven't put one bit of sugar in."

"For the land sakes!" Mrs. Little did not take correction of this kind happily, but when she was made to fairly acknowledge the need of it, she showed no resentment. She laid the upper crust back on the board and sweetened the pie. Ann Mary watched her gravely, but she was inwardly complacent. After she had rescued the pudding from being baked without the plums, and it was nearly dinner-time, her grandfather came home. He had been over to the village to buy the Thanksgiving turkey. Ann Mary looked out with delight when he drove past the windows on his way to the barn.

"Grandpa's got home," said she.

It was snowing quite hard, and she saw the old man and the steadily tramping white horse and the tilting wagon through a thick mist of falling snow-flakes.

Before Mr. Little came into the kitchen, his wife warned him to be sure to wipe all the snow from his feet, and not to track in any, so he stamped vigorously out in the shed. Then he entered with an air of pride. "There!" said he, "what do ye think of that for a turkey?" Mr. Little was generally slow and gentle in his ways, but to-day he was quite excited over the turkey. He held it up with considerable difficulty. He

MR. LITTLE SELECTS THE THANKSGIVING TURKEY

was a small old man, and the cords on his lean hands knotted. "It weighs a good fifteen pound'," said he, " an' there wasn't a better one in the store. Adkins didn't have a very big lot on hand."

"I should think that was queer, the day before Thanksgivin'," said Mrs. Little. She was examining the turkey critically. "I guess it'll do," she declared finally. That was her highest expression of approbation. "Well, I rayther thought you'd think so," rejoined the old man, beaming. "I guess it's about as good a one as can be got—they said 'twas, down there. Sam White he was in there, and he said 'twas; he said I was goin' to get it in pretty good season for Thanksgivin', he thought."

"I don't think it's such very extra season, the day before Thanksgivin'," said Mrs. Little.

"Well, I don't think 'twas, nuther. I didn't see jest what Sam meant by it."

Ann Mary was dumb with admiration. When the turkey was laid on the broad shelf in the pantry, she went and gazed upon it. In the afternoon there was great enjoyment seeing it stuffed and made ready for the oven. Indeed, this day was throughout one of great enjoyment, being full of the very aroma of festivity and good cheer and gala times, and even sweeter than the occasion which it preceded. Ann Mary had only one damper all day, and that was the non-arrival of a letter. Mrs. Little had invited her son and his family to spend Thanksgiving, but now they probably were not coming, since not a word in reply had been received. When Mr. Little said there was no letter in the post-office, Ann Mary's face fell. "Oh, dear," said she, "don't you suppose Lucy will come, grandma?"

"No," replied her grandmother, "I don't. Edward never did such a thing as not to send me word when he was comin', in his life, nor Maria neither. I ain't no idee they'll come."

"Oh, dear!" said Ann Mary again.

"Well, you'll have to make up your mind to it," returned her grandmother. She was sore over her own disappointment, and so was irascible towards Ann Mary's. "It's no worse for you than for the rest of us. I guess you can keep one Thanksgivin' without Lucy."

For a while it almost seemed to Ann Mary that she could not. Lucy was her only cousin. She loved Lucy dearly, and she was lonesome for another little girl; nobody knew how she had counted upon seeing her cousin. Ann Mary herself had a forlorn hope that Lucy still might come, even if Uncle Edward *was* always so particular about sending word, and no word had been received. On Thanksgiving morning she kept running to the window and looking down the road. But when the stage from the village came, it passed right by the house without slackening its speed.

Then there was no hope left at all.

"You might jest as well be easy," said her grandmother. "I guess you can have a good Thanksgivin' if Lucy *ain't* here. This evenin' you can ask Loretty to come over a little while, if you want to, an' you can make some nut-candy."

"Loretta ain't at home."

"She'll come home for Thanksgivin', I guess. It ain't very likely she's stayed away over that. When I get the dinner ready to take up, you can carry a plateful down to Sarah Bean's, an' that'll be somethin' for you to do, too. I guess you can manage."

Thanksgiving Day was a very pleasant day, although there was considerable snow on the ground, for it had snowed all the day before. Mr. Little and Ann Mary did not go to church as usual, on that account.

The old man did not like to drive to the village before the roads were beaten out. Mrs. Little lamented not a little over it. It was the custom for her husband and granddaughter to attend church Thanksgiving morning, while she stayed at home and cooked the dinner. "It does seem dreadful heathenish for nobody to go to meetin' Thanksgivin' Day," said she; "an' we ain't even heard the proclamation read, neither. It rained so hard last Sabbath that we couldn't go."

The season was unusually wintry and severe, and lately the family had been prevented from church-going. It was two Sundays since any of the family had gone. The village was three miles away, and the road was rough. Mr. Little was too old to drive over it in very bad weather.

When Ann Mary went to carry the plate of Thanksgiving dinner to Sarah Bean, she wore a pair of her grandfather's blue woollen socks drawn over her shoes to keep out the snow. The snow was rather deep for easy walking, but she did not mind that. She carried the dinner with great care; there was a large plate well filled, and a tin dish was turned over it to keep it warm. Sarah Bean was an old woman who lived alone. Her house was about a quarter of a mile from the Littles'.

When Ann Mary reached the house, she found the old woman making a cup of tea. There did not seem to be much of anything but tea and bread-and-butter for her dinner. She was very deaf and infirm, all her joints shook when she tried to use them, and her voice quavered when she talked. She took the plate, and her hands trembled so that the tin dish played on the plate like a clapper. "Why," said she, overjoyed, "this looks just like Thanksgiving Day, tell your grandma!"

"Why, it *is* Thanksgiving Day," declared Ann Mary, with some wonder.

"What?" asked Sarah Bean.

"*It is Thanksgiving Day, you know.*" But it was of no use, the old woman could not hear a word. Ann Mary's voice was too low.

Ann Mary could not walk very fast on account of the snow. She was absent some three-quarters of an hour; her grandmother had told her that dinner would be all on the table when she returned. She was enjoying the nice things in anticipation all the way; when she came near the house, she could smell roasted turkey, and there was also a sweet spicy odor in the air.

She noticed with surprise that a sleigh had been in the yard. "I wonder who's come," she said to herself. She thought of Lucy, and whether they *could* have driven over from the village. She ran in. "Why, who's come?" she cried out.

Her voice sounded like a shout in her own

ears; it seemed to awaken echoes. She fairly startled herself, for there was no one in the room. There was absolute quiet through all the house. There was even no sizzling from the kettles on the stove, for everything had been dished up. The vegetables, all salted and peppered and buttered, were on the table—but the turkey was not there. In the great vacant place where the turkey should have been was a piece of white paper. Ann Mary spied it in a moment. She caught it up and looked at it. It was a note from her grandmother:

We have had word that Aunt Betsey has had a bad turn. Lizz wants us to come. The dinner is all ready for you. If we ain't home to-night, you can get Loretty to stay with you. Be a good girl. GRANDMA.

Ann Mary read the note and stood reflecting, her mouth drooping at the corners. Aunt Betsey was Mrs. Little's sister; Lizz was her daughter who lived with her and took care of her. They lived in Derby, and Derby was fourteen miles away. It seemed a long distance to Ann Mary, and she felt sure that her grandparents could not come home that night. She looked around the empty room and sighed. After a while she sat down and pulled off the snowy socks; she thought she might as well eat her dinner, although she did not feel so hungry as she had expected. Everything was on the table but the turkey and plum-pudding. Ann Mary supposed these were in the oven keeping warm; the door was ajar. But, when she looked, they were not there. She went into the pantry; they were not there either. It was very strange; there was the dripping-pan in which the turkey had been baked, on the back of the stove, with some gravy in it; and there was the empty pudding-dish on the hearth.

"What has grandma done with the turkey and the plum-pudding?" said Ann Mary, aloud.

She looked again in the pantry; then she went down cellar—there seemed to be so few places in the house in which it was reasonable to search for a turkey and a plum-pudding!

Finally she gave it up, and sat down to dinner. There was plenty of squash and potatoes and turnips and onions and beets and cranberry-sauce and pies; but it was no Thanksgiving dinner without turkey and plum-pudding. It was like a great flourish of accompaniment without any song.

Ann Mary did as well as she could; she put some turkey-gravy on her potato and filled up her plate with vegetables; but she did not enjoy the dinner. She felt more and more lonely, too.

She resolved that after she had washed up the dinner dishes and changed her dress, she would go over to Loretta Adams's. It was quite a piece of work, washing the dinner dishes, there were so many pans and kettles; it was the middle of the afternoon when she finished. Then Ann Mary put on her best plaid dress, and tied her best red ribbons on her braids, and it was four o'clock before she started for Loretta's.

Loretta lived in a white cottage about half a mile away towards the village. The front yard had many bushes in it, and the front path was bordered with box; the bushes were now mounds of snow, and the box was indicated by two snowy ridges.

The house had a shut-up look; the sitting-room curtains were down. Ann Mary went around to the side door; but it was locked. Then she went up the front walk between the snowy ridges of box, and tried the front door; that also was locked. The Adamses had gone away. Ann Mary did not know what to do. The tears stood in her eyes, and she choked a little. She went back and forth between the two doors, and shook and pounded; she peeked around the corner of the curtain into the sitting-room. She could see Loretta's organ, with the music-book, and all the familiar furniture, but the room wore an utterly deserted air.

Finally, Ann Mary sat down on the front door-step, after she had brushed off the snow a little. She had made up her mind to wait a little while, and see if the folks would not come home. She had on her red hood, and her grandmother's old plaid shawl. She pulled the shawl tightly around her, and muffled her face in it; it was extremely cold weather for sitting on a door-step. Just across the road was a low clump of birches; through and above the birches the sky showed red and clear where the sun was setting. Everything looked cold and bare and desolate to the little girl who was trying to keep Thanksgiving. Suddenly she heard a little cry, and Loretta's white cat came around the corner of the house.

"Kitty, kitty, kitty," called Ann Mary. She was very fond of Loretta's cat; she had none of her own.

The cat came close and brushed around Ann Mary so she took it up in her lap; and wrapped the shawl around it, and felt a little comforted.

She sat there on the door-step and held the cat until it was quite dusky, and she was very stiff with the cold. Then she put down the cat and prepared to go home. But she had not gone far along the road when she found out that the cat was following her. The little white creature floundered through the snow at her heels, and mewed constantly. Sometimes it darted ahead and waited until she came up, but it did not seem willing to be carried in her arms.

When Ann Mary reached her own house the lonesome look of it sent a chill all over her; she was afraid to go in. She made up her mind to go down to Sarah Bean's and ask whether she could not stay all night there.

So she kept on, and Loretta's white cat still followed her. There was no light in Sarah Bean's house. Ann Mary knocked and pounded, but it was of no use; the old woman had gone to bed, and she could not make her hear.

Ann Mary turned about and went home; the tears were running down her cold red cheeks. The cat mewed louder than ever. When she got home she took the cat up and carried it into the house. She determined to keep it for company, anyway. She was sure, now, that she would have to stay alone all night; the Adamses and Sarah Bean were the only neighbors, and it was so late now that she had no hope of her grandparents' return. Ann Mary was timid and nervous, but she had a vein of philosophy, and she generally grasped the situation with all the strength she had, when she became convinced that she must. She had laid her plans while walking home through the keen winter air, even as the tears were streaming over her cheeks, and she proceeded to carry them into execution. She gave Loretta's cat its supper, and she ate a piece of mince-pie herself; then she fixed the kitchen and the sitting-room fires, and locked up the house very thoroughly. Next, she took the cat and the lamp and went into the dark bedroom and locked the door; then she and the cat were as safe as she knew how to make them. The dark bedroom was in the very middle of the house, the centre of a nest of rooms. It was small and square, had no windows, and only one door. It was a sort of fastness. Ann Mary made up her mind that she would not undress herself, and that she would keep the lamp burning all night. She climbed into the big yellow-posted bedstead, and the cat cuddled up to her and purred.

Ann Mary lay in bed and stared at the white satin scrolls on the wall-paper, and listened for noises. She heard a great many, but they were all mysterious and indefinable, till about ten o'clock. Then she sat straight up in bed and her heart beat fast. She certainly heard sleigh-bells; the sound penetrated even to the dark bedroom. Then came a jarring pounding on the side door.

Ann Mary got up, unfastened the bedroom door, took the lamp, and stepped out into the sitting-room. The pounding came again. "Ann Mary, Ann Mary!" cried a voice. It was her grandmother's.

"I'm comin', I'm comin', grandma!" shouted Ann Mary. She had never felt so happy in her life. She pushed back the bolt of the side door with trembling haste. There stood her grandmother all muffled up, with a shawl over her head; and out in the yard were her grandfather and another man, with a horse and sleigh. The men were turning the sleigh around.

"Put the lamp in the window, Ann Mary," called Mr. Little, and Ann Mary obeyed. Her grandmother sank into a chair. "I'm jest about tuckered out," she groaned. "If I don't ketch my death with this day's work, I'm lucky. There ain't any more feelin' in my feet than as if they was lumps of stone."

Ann Mary stood at her grandmother's elbow, and her face was all beaming. "I thought you weren't coming," said she.

"Well, I shouldn't have come a step to-night, if it hadn't been for you—and the cow," said her grandmother, in an indignant voice. "I was kind of uneasy about you, an' we knew the cow wouldn't be milked unless you got Mr. Adams to come over."

"Was Aunt Betsey very sick?" inquired Ann Mary.

Her grandmother gave her head a toss. "Sick! No, there wa'n't a thing the matter with her, except she ate some sassage-meat, an' had a little faint turn. Lizz was scart to death, the way she always is. She didn't act as if she knew whether her head was on, all the time we were there. She didn't act as if she knew 'twas Thanksgivin' Day; an' she didn't have no turkey that I could see. Aunt Betsey bein' took sick seemed to put everythin' out of her head. I never saw such a nervous thing as she is. I was all out of patience when I got there. Betsey didn't seem to be very bad off, an' there we'd hurried enough to break our necks. We didn't dare to drive around to Sarah Bean's to let you know about it, for we was afraid we'd miss the train. We jest got in with the man that brought the word, an' he driv as fast as he could over to the village, an' then we lost the train, an' had to sit there in the depot two mortal hours. An' now we've come fourteen mile' in an open sleigh. The man that lives next door to Betsey said he'd bring us home, an' I thought we'd better come. He's goin' over to the village to-night; he's got folks there. I told him he'd a good deal better stay here, but he won't. He's as deaf as an adder, an' you can't make him hear anythin', anyway. We ain't spoke a word all the way home. Where's Loretty? She came over to stay with you, didn't she?"

Ann Mary explained that Loretta was not at home.

"That's queer, seems to me, Thanksgivin' Day," said her grandmother. "Massy sakes, what cat's that? She came out of the settin'-room!"

Ann Mary explained about Loretta's cat. Then she burst forth with the question that had been uppermost in her mind ever since her grandmother came in. "Grandma," said she, "what did you do with the turkey and the plum-pudding?"

"What?"

"What did you do with the turkey and the plum-pudding?"

"The turkey an' the plum-puddin'?"

"Yes; I couldn't find 'em anywhere."

Mrs. Little, who had removed her wraps, and was crouching over the kitchen stove with her feet in the oven, looked at Ann Mary with a dazed expression.

"I dunno what you mean, child," said she.

Mr. Little had helped the man with the sleigh to start, and had now come in. He was pulling off his boots.

"Don't you remember, mother," said he, "how you run back in the house, an' said you was goin' to set that turkey an' plum-pudding away, for you was afraid to leave 'em settin' right out in plain sight on the table, for fear that somebody might come in?"

"Yes; I do remember," said Mrs. Little. "I thought they looked 'most too temptin'. I set 'em in the pantry. I thought Ann Mary could get 'em when she came in."

"They ain't in the pantry," said Ann Mary.

Her grandmother arose and went into the pantry with a masterful air. "Ain't in the pantry?" she repeated. "I don't s'pose you more'n gave one look."

Ann Mary followed her grandmother. She fairly expected to see the turkey and pudding before her eyes on the shelf and to admit that she had been mistaken. Mr. Little also followed, and they all stood in the pantry and looked about.

"I guess they ain't here, mother," said Mr. Little. "Can't you think where you set 'em?"

The old woman took up the lamp and stepped out of the pantry with dignity. "I've set 'em somewhere," said she, in a curt voice, "an' I'll find 'em in the mornin'. You don't want any turkey or plum-puddin' to-night, neither of you!"

But Mrs. Little did not find the turkey and the plum-pudding in the morning. Some days went by, and their whereabouts was as much a mystery as ever. Mrs. Little could not remember where she had put them; but it had been in some secure hiding-place, since her own wit which had placed them there could not find it out. She was so mortified and worried over it that she was nearly ill. She tried to propound the theory, and believe in it herself, that she had really set the turkey and the pudding in the pantry, and that they had been stolen; but she was too honest. "I've heerd of folks puttin' things in such safe places that they couldn't find 'em, before now," said she; "but I never heerd of losin' a turkey an' a plum-puddin' that way. I dunno but I'm losin' what little wits I ever did have." She went about with a humble and resentful air. She promised Ann Mary that she would cook another turkey and pudding the first of the week, if the missing ones were not found.

Sunday came and they were not discovered. It was a pleasant day, and the Littles went to the village church. Ann Mary looked over across the church after they were seated and saw Loretta, with the pretty brown frizzes over her forehead, sitting between her father and mother, and she wondered when Loretta had come home.

The choir sang and the minister prayed. Suddenly Ann Mary saw him, standing there in the pulpit, unfold a paper. Then *the minister began to read the Thanksgiving Proclamation.* Ann Mary cast one queer glance at her grandmother, who returned it with one of inexpressible dignity and severity.

As soon as meeting was done, her grandmother clutched her by the arm. "Don't you say a word about it to anybody," she whispered. "You mind!"

When they were in the sleigh going home she charged her husband. "You mind, you keep still, father," said she. "It 'll be town-talk if you don't."

The old man chuckled. "Don't you know, I said once that I had kind of an idee that Thanksgivin' weren't quite so early, and you shut me up, mother," he remarked. He looked good-naturedly malicious.

"Well, I dunno as it's anything so very queer," said Mrs. Little. "It comes a whole week later than it did last year, and I s'posed we'd missed hearin' the proclamation."

The next day a letter arrived saying that Lucy and her father and mother were coming to spend

Thanksgiving. "I feel jest about beat," Mrs. Little said, when she read the letter.

Really, she did feel about at her wit's end. The turkey and pudding were not yet found, and she had made up her mind that she would not dare wait much longer without providing more. She knew that another turkey must be procured, at all events. However, she waited until the last minute Wednesday afternoon, then she went to work mixing a pudding. Mr. Little had gone to the store for the turkey. "Sam White was over there, an' he said he thought we was goin' right into turkeys this year," he reported when he got home.

That night the guests arrived. Thanksgiving morning Lucy and Ann Mary and their grandfather and Lucy's father and mother were all going to meeting. Mrs. Little was to stay at home and cook the dinner.

Thanksgiving morning Mr. Little made a fire in the best parlor air-tight stove, and just before they started for meeting Lucy and Ann Mary were in the room. Lucy, in the big rocking-chair that was opposite the sofa, was rocking to and fro and talking. Ann Mary sat near the window. Each of the little girls had on her coat and hat.

Suddenly Lucy stopped rocking and looked intently over towards the sofa.

"What you lookin' at, Lucy?" asked Ann Mary, curiously.

Lucy still looked. "Why—I was wondering what was under that sofa," said she, slowly. Then she turned to Ann Mary, and her face was quite pale and startled—she had heard the turkey and pudding story. "Oh, Ann Mary, it does look—like—oh—"

Both little girls rushed to the sofa, and threw themselves on the floor. "Oh, oh, oh!" they shrieked. "Grandma—mother! Come quick, come quick!"

When the others came in, there sat Ann Mary and Lucy on the floor, and between them were the turkey and the plum-pudding, each carefully covered with a snow-white napkin.

Mrs. Little was quite pale and trembling. "I remember now," said she, faintly, "I run in here with 'em."

She was so overcome that the others tried to take it quietly and not to laugh much. But every little while, after Lucy and Ann Mary were seated in church, they would look at each other and have to put their handkerchiefs to their faces. However, Ann Mary tried hard to listen to the sermon, and to behave well. In the depths of her childish heart she felt grateful and happy. There, by her side, sat her dear Lucy, whose sweet little face peeped out from a furry winter hat. Just across the aisle was Loretta, who was coming in the evening, and then they would pop corn and make nut-candy. At home there was the beautiful new turkey and unlimited pudding and good cheer, and all disappointment and mystery were done away with.

Ann Mary felt as if all her troubles would be followed by thanksgivings.

ANN LIZY'S PATCHWORK

Ann Lizy was invited to spend the afternoon and take tea with her friend Jane Baxter, and she was ready to set forth about one o'clock. That was the fashionable hour for children and their elders to start when they were invited out to spend the afternoon.

Ann Lizy had on her best muslin delaine dress, her best embroidered pantalets, her black silk apron, and her flat straw hat with long blue ribbon streamers. She stood in the south room—the sitting-room—before her grandmother, who was putting some squares of patchwork, with needle, thread, and scissors, into a green silk bag embroidered with roses in bead-work.

"There, Ann Lizy," said her grandmother, "you may take my bag if you are real careful of it, and won't lose it. When you get to Jane's you lay it on the table, and don't have it round when you're playin' out-doors."

"Yes, ma'am," said Ann Lizy. She was looking with radiant, admiring eyes at the bag—its cluster of cunningly wrought pink roses upon the glossy green field of silk. Still there was a serious droop to her mouth; she knew there was a bitter to this sweet.

"Now," said her grandmother, "I've put four squares of patchwork in the bag; they're all cut and basted nice, and you must sew 'em all, over and over, before you play any. Sew 'em real fine and even, or you'll have to pick the stitches out when you get home."

Ann Lizy's radiant eyes faded; she hung her head. She calculated swiftly that she could not finish the patchwork before four o'clock, and that would leave her only an hour and a half to eat supper and play with Jane, for she would have to come home at half-past five. "Can't I take two, and do the other two to-morrow, grandma?" said she.

Her grandmother straightened herself disapprovingly. She was a tall, wiry old woman with strong, handsome features showing through her wrinkles. She had been so energetic all her life, and done so much work, that her estimation of it was worn, like scales. Four squares of patchwork sewed with very fine even stitches had, to her, no weight at all; it did not seem like work.

"Well, if a great girl like you can't sew four squares of patchwork in an arternoon, I wouldn't tell of it, Ann Lizy," said she. "I don't know what you'd say if you had to work the way I did at your age. If you can't have time enough to play and do a little thing like that, you'd better stay at home. I ain't goin' to have you idle a whole arternoon, if I know it. Time's worth too much to be wasted that way."

"I'd sew the others to-morrow," pleaded Ann Lizy, faintly.

"Oh, you wouldn't do it half so easy to-morrow; you've got to pick the currants for the jell' to-morrow. Besides, that doesn't make any difference. To-day's work is to-day's work, and it hasn't anything to do with to-morrow's. It's no excuse for idlin' one day, because you do work the next. You take that patchwork, and sit right down and sew it as soon as you get there —don't put it off—and sew it nice, too, or you can stay at home—just which you like."

Ann Lizy sighed, but reached out her hand for the bag. "Now be careful and not lose it," said her grandmother, "and be a good girl."

"Yes, ma'am."

"Don't run too hard, nor go to climbin' walls, and get your best dress torn."

"No, ma'am."

"And only one piece of cake at tea-time."

"Yes, ma'am."

"And start for home at half-past five."

"Yes, ma'am."

Little Ann Lizy Jennings, as she went down the walk between the rows of pinks, had a bewildered feeling that she had been to Jane Baxter's to tea, and was home again.

Her parents were dead, and she lived with her Grandmother Jennings, who made her childhood comfortable and happy, except that at times she seemed taken off her childish feet by the energy and strong mind of the old woman, and so swung a little way through the world in her wake. But Ann Lizy received no harm by it.

Ann Lizy went down the road with the bead bag on her arm. She toed out primly, for she had on her best shoes. A little girl, whom she knew, stood at the gate in every-day clothes, and Ann Lizy bowed to her in the way she had seen the parson's wife bow, when out making calls in her best black silk and worked lace veil. The parson's wife was young and pretty, and Ann Lizy admired her. It was quite a long walk to Jane Baxter's, but it was a beautiful afternoon, and the road was pleasant, although there were not many houses. There were green fields and flowering bushes at the sides, and, some of the way, elm-trees arching over it. Ann Lizy would have been very happy had it not been for the patchwork. She had already pieced one patchwork quilt, and her grandmother displayed it to people with pride, saying, "Ann Lizy pieced that before she was eight years old."

Ann Lizy had not as much ambition as her grandmother, now she was engaged upon her second quilt, and it looked to her like a checked and besprigged calico mountain. She kept dwelling upon those four squares, over and over, until she felt as if each side were as long as the Green Mountains. She calculated again and again how little time she would have to play with Jane — only about an hour, for she must allow a half-hour for tea. She was not a swift sewer when she sewed fine and even stitches, and she knew she could not finish those squares before four o'clock. One hour!—and she and Jane wanted to play dolls, and make wreaths out of oak-leaves, and go down in the lane after thimbleberries, and in the garden for gooseberries—there would be no time for anything!

Ann Lizy's delicate little face under the straw flat grew more and more sulky and distressed, her forehead wrinkled, and her mouth pouted. She forgot to swing her muslin delaine skirts gracefully, and flounced along hitting the dusty meadowsweet bushes.

Ann Lizy was about half-way to Jane Baxter's house, in a lonely part of the road, when she opened her bead bag and drew out her pocket-handkerchief—her grandmother had tucked that in with the patchwork—and wiped her eyes. When she replaced the handkerchief she put it under the patchwork, and did not draw up the bag again, but went on, swinging it violently by one string.

When Ann Lizy reached Jane Baxter's gate she gave a quick, scared glance at the bag. It looked very flat and limp. She did not open it, and she said nothing about it to Jane. They went out to play in the garden. There were so many hollyhocks there that it seemed like a real flower-grove, and the gooseberries were ripe.

Shortly after Ann Lizy entered Jane Baxter's house a white horse and a chaise passed down the road in the direction from which she had just come. There were three persons in the chaise—a gentleman, lady, and little girl. The lady wore a green silk pelerine, and a green bonnet with pink strings, and the gentleman a blue coat and bell hat. The little girl had pretty long, light curls, and wore a white dress and blue sash. She sat on a little footstool down in front of the seat. They were the parson's wife's sister, her husband, and her little girl, and had been to visit at the parsonage. The gentleman drove the white horse down the road, and the little girl looked sharply and happily at everything by the way. All at once she gave a little cry—"Oh, father, what's that in the road?"

She saw Ann Lizy's patchwork, all four squares nicely pinned together, lying beside the meadow-sweet bushes. Her father stopped the horse, got out, and picked up the patchwork.

"Why," said the parson's wife's sister, "some little girl has lost her patchwork; look, Sally!"

"She'll be sorry, won't she?" said the little girl, whose name was Sally.

The gentleman got back into the chaise, and the three rode off with the patchwork. There seemed to be nothing else to do; there were no houses near and no people of whom to inquire. Besides, four squares of calico patchwork were not especially valuable.

"If we don't find out who lost it, I'll put it into my quilt," said Sally. She studied the patterns of the calico very happily, as they rode along; she thought them prettier than anything she had. One had pink roses on a green ground, and she thought that especially charming.

Meantime, while Sally and her father **and**

mother rode away in the chaise with the patchwork to Whitefield, ten miles distant, where their house was, Ann Lizy and Jane played as fast as they could. It was four o'clock before they went into the house. Ann Lizy opened her bag, which she had laid on the parlor table with the *Young Lady's Annuals* and *Mrs. Hemans's Poems*. "I s'pose I must sew my patchwork," said she, in a miserable, guilty little voice. Then she exclaimed. It was strange that, well as she knew there was no patchwork there, the actual discovery of nothing at all gave her a shock.

"What's the matter?" asked Jane.

"I've—lost my patchwork," said Ann Lizy.

Jane called her mother, and they condoled with Ann Lizy. Ann Lizy sat in one of Mrs. Baxter's rush-bottomed chairs and began to cry.

"Where did you lose it?" Mrs. Baxter asked. "Don't cry, Ann Lizy, maybe we can find it."

"I s'pose I—lost it comin'," sobbed Ann Lizy.

"Well, I'll tell you what 't is," said Mrs. Baxter; "you and Jane had better run up the road a piece, and likely as not you'll find it; and I'll have tea all ready when you come home. Don't feel so bad, child, you'll find it, right where you dropped it."

But Ann Lizy and Jane, searching carefully along the road, did not find the patchwork where it had been dropped. "Maybe it's blown away," suggested Jane, although there was hardly wind enough that afternoon to stir a feather. And the two little girls climbed over the stone-walls and searched in the fields, but they did not find the patchwork. Then another mishap befell Ann Lizy. She tore a three-cornered place in her best muslin delaine, getting over the wall. When she saw that she felt as if she were in a dreadful dream. "Oh, what will grandma say!" she wailed.

"Maybe she won't scold," said Jane, consolingly.

"Yes, she will. Oh dear!"

The two little girls went dolefully home to tea. There were hot biscuits and honey and tarts and short gingerbread and custards, but Ann Lizy did not feel hungry. Mrs. Baxter tried to comfort her; she really saw not much to mourn over, except the rent in the best dress, as four squares of patchwork could easily be replaced; she did not see the true inwardness of the case.

At half-past five, Ann Lizy, miserable and tear-stained, the three-cornered rent in her best dress pinned up, started for home, and then—her grandmother's beautiful bead bag was not to be found. Ann Lizy and Jane both remembered that it had been carried when they set out to find the patchwork. Ann Lizy had meditated bringing the patchwork home in it.

"Aunt Cynthy made that bag for grandma," said Ann Lizy, in a tone of dull despair; this was beyond tears.

"Well, Jane shall go with you, and help find it," said Mrs. Baxter, "and I'll leave the tea-dishes and go too. Don't feel so bad, Ann Lizy, I know I can find it."

But Mrs. Baxter and Jane and Ann Lizy, all searching, could not find the bead bag. "My best handkerchief was in it," said Ann Lizy. It seemed to her as if all her best things were gone. She and Mrs. Baxter and Jane made a doleful little group in the road. The frogs were peeping, and the cows were coming home. Mrs. Baxter asked the boy who drove the cows if he had seen a green bead bag, or four squares of patchwork; he stared and shook his head.

Ann Lizy looked like a wilted meadow reed, the blue streamers on her hat drooped dejectedly, her best shoes were all dusty, and the three-cornered rent was the feature of her best muslin delaine dress that one saw first. Then her little delicate face was all tear-stains and downward curves. She stood there in the road as if she had not courage to stir.

"Now, Ann Lizy," said Mrs. Baxter, "you'd

better run right home and not worry. I don't believe your grandma 'll scold you when you tell her just how 't was."

Ann Lizy shook her head. "Yes, she will."

"Well, she'll be worrying about you if you ain't home before long, and I guess you'd better go," said Mrs. Baxter.

Ann Lizy said not another word; she began to move dejectedly towards home. Jane and her mother called many kindly words after her, but she did not heed them. She kept straight on, walking slowly until she was home. Her grandmother stood in the doorway watching for her. She had a blue-yarn stocking in her hands, and she was knitting fast as she watched.

"Ann Lizy, where have you been, late as this?" she called out, as Ann Lizy came up the walk. "It's arter six o'clock."

Ann Lizy continued to drag herself slowly forward, but she made no reply.

"Why don't you speak?"

Ann Lizy crooked her arm around her face and began to cry. Her grandmother reached down, took her by the shoulder, and led her into the house. "What on airth is the matter, child?" said she; "have you fell down?"

"No, ma'am."

"What does ail you, then? Ann Lizy Jennings, how come that great three-cornered tear in your best dress?"

Ann Lizy sobbed.

"Answer me."

"I—tore it gittin' over—the wall."

"What were you gettin' over walls for in your best dress? I'd like to know what you s'pose you'll have to wear to meetin' now. Didn't I tell you not to get over walls in your best dress? *Ann Lizy Jennings, where is my bead bag?*"

"I—lost it."

"Lost my bead bag?"

"Yes, ma'am."

"How did you lose it, eh?"

"I lost it when—I was lookin' for—my patchwork."

"Did you lose your patchwork?"

"Yes, ma'am."

"When?"

"When I was—goin' over to—Jane's."

"Lost it out of the bag?"

Ann Lizy nodded, sobbing.

"Then you went to look for it and lost the bag. Lost your best pocket-handkerchief, too?"

"Yes, ma'am."

Old Mrs. Jennings stood looking at Ann Lizy.

"All that patchwork, cut out and basted jest as nice as could be, your best pocket-handkerchief and my bead bag lost, and your meetin' dress tore," said she; "well, you've done about enough for one day. Take off your things and go up-stairs to bed. You can't go over to Jane Baxter's again for one spell, and every mite of the patchwork that goes into the quilt you've got to cut by a thread, and baste yourself, and to-morrow you've got to hunt for that patchwork and that bag till you find 'em, if it takes you all day. Go right along."

Ann Lizy took off her hat and climbed meekly up-stairs and went to bed. She did not say her prayers; she lay there and wept. It was about half-past eight, the air coming through the open window was loud with frogs and katydids and whippoorwills, and the twilight was very deep, when Ann Lizy arose and crept down-stairs. She could barely see her way.

There was a candle lighted in the south room, and her grandmother sat there knitting. Ann Lizy, a piteous little figure in her white nightgown, stood in the door.

"Well, what is it?" her grandmother said, in a severe voice that had a kindly inflection in it.

"Grandma—"

"What is it?"

"I lost my patchwork on purpose. I didn't want—to sew it."

"Lost your patchwork on purpose!"

"Yes—ma'am," sobbed Ann Lizy.

"Let it drop out of the bag on purpose?"

"Yes, ma'am."

"Well, you did a dreadful wicked thing then. Go right back to bed."

Ann Lizy went back to bed and to sleep. Remorse no longer gnawed keenly enough at her clear, childish conscience to keep her awake, now her sin was confessed. She said her prayers and went to sleep. Although the next morning the reckoning came, the very worst punishment was over for her. Her grandmother held the judicious use of the rod to be a part of her duty towards her beloved little orphan granddaughter, so she switched Ann Lizy with a little rod of birch, and sent her forth full of salutary tinglings to search for the bead bag and the patchwork. All the next week Ann Lizy searched the fields and road for the missing articles, when she was not cutting calico patchwork by a thread and sewing over and over. It seemed to her that life was made up of those two occupations, but at the end of a week the search, so far as the bead bag was concerned, came to an end.

On Saturday afternoon the parson's wife called on old Mrs. Jennings. The sweet, gentle young lady in her black silk dress, her pink cheeks, and smooth waves of golden hair gleaming through her worked lace veil entered the north room, which was the parlor, and sat down in the rocking-chair. Ann Lizy and her grandmother sat opposite, and they both noticed at the same moment that the parson's wife held in her hand—*the bead bag!*

Ann Lizy gave a little involuntary "oh;" her grandmother shook her head fiercely at her, and the parson's wife noticed nothing. She went on talking about the pinks out in the yard, in her lovely low voice.

As soon as she could, old Mrs. Jennings excused herself and beckoned Ann Lizy to follow her out of the room. Then, while she was arranging a square of pound-cake and a little glass of elderberry wine on a tray, she charged Ann Lizy to say nothing about the bead bag to the parson's wife. "Mind you act as if you didn't see it," said she; "don't sit there lookin' at it that way."

"But it's your bead bag, grandma," said Ann Lizy, in a bewildered way.

"Don't you say anything," admonished her grandmother. "Now carry this tray in, and be careful you don't spill the elderberry wine."

Poor Ann Lizy tried her best not to look at the bead bag, while the parson's wife ate pound-cake, sipped the elderberry wine, and conversed in her sweet, gracious way; but it did seem finally to her as if it were the bead bag instead of the parson's wife that was making the call. She kept wondering if the parson's wife would not say, "Mrs. Jennings, is this your bead bag?" but she did not. She made the call and took leave, and the bead bag was never mentioned. It was odd, too, that it was not; for the parson's wife, who had found the bead bag, had taken it with her on her round of calls that afternoon, partly to show it and find out, if she could, who had lost it. But here it was driven out of her mind by the pound-cake and elderberry wine, or else she did not think it likely that an old lady like Mrs. Jennings could have owned the bag. Younger ladies than she usually carried them. However it was, she went away with the bag.

"Why didn't she ask if it was yours?" inquired Ann Lizy, indignant in spite of her admiration for the parson's wife.

"Hush," said her grandmother. "You mind you don't say a word out about this, Ann Lizy. I ain't never carried it, and she didn't suspect."

Now, the bead bag was found after this unsatisfactory fashion; but Ann Lizy never went down the road without looking for the patchwork. She never dreamed how little Sally Putnam, the minister's wife's niece, was in the meantime sewing these four squares over and over, getting them ready to go into her quilt. It was a month later before she found it out, and it was strange that she discovered it at all.

It so happened that, one afternoon in the last of August, old Mrs. Jennings dressed herself in her best black bombazine, her best bonnet and mantilla and mitts, and also dressed Ann Lizy in her best muslin delaine, exquisitely mended, and set out to make a call on the parson's wife. When they arrived they found a chaise and white horse out in the parsonage yard, and the parson's wife's sister and family there on a visit. An old lady, Mrs. White, a friend of Mrs. Jennings, was also making a call.

Little Ann Lizy and Sally Putnam were introduced to each other, and Ann Lizy looked admiringly at Sally's long curls and low-necked dress, which had gold catches in the sleeves. They sat and smiled shyly at each other.

"Show Ann Lizy your patchwork, Sally," the parson's wife said, presently. "Sally has got almost enough patchwork for a quilt, and she has brought it over to show me," she added.

Ann Lizy colored to her little slender neck; patchwork was nowadays a sore subject with her, but she looked on as Sally, proud and smiling, displayed her patchwork.

Suddenly she gave a little cry. There was one of her squares! The calico with roses on a green ground was in Sally's patchwork.

Her grandmother shook her head energetically at her, but old Mrs. White had on her spectacles, and she, too, had spied the square.

"Why, Miss Jennings," she cried, "that's jest like that dress you had so long ago!"

"Let me see," said Sally's mother, quickly. "Why, yes; that is the very square you found, Sally. That is one; there were four of them, all cut and basted. Why, this little girl didn't lose them, did she?"

Then it all came out. The parson's wife was quick-witted, and she thought of the bead bag. Old Mrs. Jennings was polite, and said it did not matter; but when she and Ann Lizy went home they had the bead bag, with the patchwork and the best pocket-handkerchief in it.

It had been urged that little Sally Putnam should keep the patchwork, since she had sewed it, but her mother was not willing.

"No," said she, "this poor little girl lost it, and Sally mustn't keep it; it wouldn't be right."

Suddenly Ann Lizy straightened herself. Her

cheeks were blazing red, but her black eyes were brave.

"I lost that patchwork on purpose," said she. "I didn't want to sew it. Then I lost the bag while I was lookin' for it."

There was silence for a minute.

"You are a good girl to tell of it," said Sally's mother, finally.

Ann Lizy's grandmother shook her head meaningly at Mrs. Putnam.

"I don't know about that," said she. "Ownin'-up takes away *some* of the sin, but it don't *all*."

But when she and Ann Lizy were on their homeward road she kept glancing down at her granddaughter's small face. It struck her that it was not so plump and rosy as it had been.

"I think you've had quite a lesson by this time about that patchwork," she remarked.

"Yes, ma'am," said Ann Lizy.

They walked a little farther. The golden-rod and the asters were in blossom now, and the road was bordered with waving fringes of blue and gold. They came in sight of Jane Baxter's house.

"You may stop in Jane Baxter's, if you want to," said old Mrs. Jennings, "and ask her mother if she can come over and spend the day with you to-morrow. And tell her I say she'd better not bring her sewing, and she'd better not wear her best dress, for you and she ain't goin' to sew any, and mebbe you'll like to go berryin,' and play out-doors."

THE LITTLE PERSIAN PRINCESS

"And you must spin faster, Dorothy, or you'll go to bed without your supper," said Dame Betsy.

"Yes, ma'am," replied Dorothy. Then she twirled the wheel so fast that the spokes were a blur.

Dorothy was a pretty little girl. She had a small pink-and-white face; her hair was closely cropped and looked like a little golden cap, and her eyes were as blue as had been the flowers of the flax which she was spinning. She wore an indigo-blue frock, and she looked very short and slight beside the wheel.

Dorothy spun, Dame Betsy tended a stew-kettle that was hanging from the crane in the fireplace, and the eldest of Dame Betsy's six daughters sat on the bench beside the cottage door and ate honey-cakes. The other daughters had arrayed themselves in their best tuckers and plumed hats and farthingales, spread their ruffled parasols, and gone to walk.

Dame Betsy had wished the oldest daughter to go with her sisters; but she was rather indolent, so she dressed herself in her best, and sat down on the bench beside the door, with a plate of honey-cakes of which she was very fond. She held up her parasol to shield her face, and also to display the parasol. It was covered with very bright green satin, and had a wreath of pink roses for a border. The sun shone directly into the cottage, and the row of pewter plates on the dresser glittered; one could see them through the doorway. The front yard of Dame Betsy's cottage was like a little grove with lemon-color and pink hollyhocks; one had to look directly up the path to see the eldest daughter sitting on the bench eating honey-cakes. She was a very homely girl. All Dame Betsy's daughters were so plain and ill-tempered that they had no suitors, although they walked abroad every day.

Dame Betsy placed her whole dependence upon the linen chests when she planned to marry her daughters. At the right of her cottage stretched a great field of flax that looked now like a blue sea, and it rippled like a sea when the wind struck it. Dame Betsy and Dorothy made the flax into linen for the daughters' dowries. They had already two great chests of linen apiece, and they were to have chests filled until there were enough to attract suitors. Every little while Dame Betsy invited all the neighboring housewives to tea; then she opened the chests and unrolled the shining lengths of linen, perfumed with lavender and rosemary. "My dear daughters will have all this, and more also, when they marry," she would remark. The housewives would go home and mention it to their sons, for they themselves were tempted by the beautiful linen; but there it would end. The sons would not go to woo Dame Betsy's homely, ill-natured daughters.

Dorothy spun as fast as she was able; Dame Betsy kept a sharp watch upon her as she stirred the stew. Dorothy wanted some of the stew for her supper. It had a delicious odor, and she was very faint and hungry. She did not have a great deal to eat at any time, as she lived principally upon the scraps from the table, and the daughters were all large eaters. She also worked very hard, and never had any time to play. She was a poor child whom Dame Betsy had taken from the almshouse, and she had no relatives but an old grandmother. She had very few kind words said to her during the day, and she used often to cry herself to sleep at night.

Presently Dame Betsy went down to the store to buy some pepper to put in the stew, but as she went out of the door she spoke to the eldest daughter, and told her to go into the house and mend a rent in her apron. "Since you were too lazy to go to walk with your sisters you must go into the house and mend your apron," said she. The eldest daughter pouted, but she made no reply. Just as soon as her mother was out of hearing she called Dorothy. "Dorothy, come here a minute!" she cried, imperatively. Dorothy left her wheel and went to the door. "Look here," said the eldest daughter, "I have one honey-cake left, and I have eaten all I want. I will give you this if you will mend my apron for me."

Dorothy eyed the honey-cake wistfully, but she replied that she did not dare to leave her spinning to mend the apron.

"Why can't you mend it in the night?" asked the eldest daughter.

"I will do that," replied Dorothy, eagerly, and she held out her hand for the honey-cake. Just as she did so she saw the little boy that lived next door peeping through his fence. His beautiful little face, with his red cheeks and black eyes, looked, through the pickets, like a damask-rose. Dorothy ran swiftly over to him with her honey-cake. "You shall have half of it," said she, and she quickly broke the cake in halves, and gave one of them to the little boy. He lived with his old grandmother, and they were very poor; it was hard for them to get the coarsest porridge to eat. The little boy often stood looking through the fence and smiling at Dorothy, and the old grandmother spoke kindly to her whenever she had an opportunity.

The little boy stood on one side of the fence and Dorothy on the other, and they ate the honey-cake. Then Dorothy ran back to the house and fell to spinning again. She spun so fast, to make up for the lost time, that one could not see the wheel-spokes at all, and the room hummed like a hive of bees. But, fast as she spun, Dame Betsy, when she returned, discovered that she had been idling, and said that she must go without her supper. Poor Dorothy could not help weeping as she twirled the wheel, she was so hungry, and the honey-cake had been very small.

Dame Betsy dished up the stew and put the spoons and bowls on the table, and soon the five absent daughters came home, rustling their flounces and flirting their parasols.

They all sat down to the table and began to eat, while Dorothy stood at her wheel and sadly spun.

They had eaten all the stew except a little,

just about enough for a cat, when a little shadow fell across the floor.

"Why, who's coming?" whispered Dame Betsy, and directly all the daughters began to smooth their front hair; each thought it might be a suitor.

But everything that they could see entering the door was a beautiful gray cat. She came stepping across the floor with a dainty, velvet tread. She had a tail like a plume, and she trailed it on the floor as she walked; her fur was very soft and long, and caught the light like silver; she had delicate tufted ears, and her shining eyes were like yellow jewels.

"It's nothing but a cat!" cried the daughters in disgust, and Dame Betsy arose to get the broom; she hated cats. That decided the daughters; they also hated cats, but they liked to oppose their mother. So they insisted on keeping the cat.

There was much wrangling, but the daughters were too much for Dame Betsy; the beautiful cat was allowed to remain on the hearth, and the remnant of the stew was set down there for her. But, to every one's amazement, she refused to touch it. She sat purring, with her little silvery paws folded, her plumy tail swept gracefully around her, and quite ignored the stew.

"I will take it up and give it to the pig," said Dame Betsy.

"No, no!" cried the daughters; "leave it, and perhaps she will eat it by-and-by."

So the stew was left upon the hearth. In the excitement Dorothy had stopped spinning, and nobody had observed it. Suddenly Dame Betsy noticed that the wheel was silent.

"Why are you not spinning, miss?" she asked, sharply. "Are you stopping work to look at a cat?"

But Dorothy made no reply; she paid no attention whatever: she continued to stare at the cat; she was quite pale, and her blue eyes were very large. And no wonder, for she saw, instead of a cat, a beautiful little princess, with eyes like stars, in a trailing robe of gray velvet covered with silver embroidery, and instead of a purr she heard a softly-hummed song. Dame Betsy seized Dorothy by the arm.

"To your work!" she cried.

And Dorothy began to spin; but she was trembling from head to foot, and every now and then she glanced at the princess on the hearth.

The daughters, in their best gowns, sat with their mother around the hearth until nine o'clock; then Dorothy was ordered to leave her wheel, the cottage was locked up, and everybody went to bed

Dorothy's bed was a little bundle of straw up in the garret under the eaves. She was very tired when she lay down, but did not dare to sleep, for she remembered her promise to mend the eldest daughter's apron. So she waited until the house was still; then she arose and crept softly down-stairs.

The fire on the hearth was still burning, and there sat the princess, and the sweet hum of her singing filled the room. But Dorothy could not understand a word of the song, because it was in the Persian language. She stood in the doorway and trembled; she did not know what to do. It seemed to her that she must be losing her wits to see a princess where every one else saw a cat. Still she could not doubt the evidence of her own eyes. Finally she advanced a little way and courtesied very low. The princess stopped singing at once. She arose in a stately fashion, and fastened her bright eyes upon Dorothy.

"So you know me?" said she.

Dorothy courtesied again.

"Are you positive that I am not a cat?"

Dorothy courtesied.

"Well, I am *not* a cat," said the princess. "I am a true princess from Persia, travelling incognita. You are the first person who has pierced my disguise. You must have very extraordinary eyes. Aren't you hungry?"

Dorothy courtesied.

"Come here and eat the stew," ordered the princess, in a commanding tone. "Meantime I will cook my own supper."

With that the princess gave a graceful leap across the floor; her gray velvet robe fluttered like a gray wing. Dorothy saw a little mouse scud before her; then in an instant the princess had him! But the moment the princess lifted the mouse, he became a gray pigeon, all dressed for cooking.

The princess sat down on the hearth and put the pigeon on the coals to broil.

"You had better eat your stew," said she; "I won't offer you any of this pigeon, because you could not help suspecting it was mouse."

So Dorothy timidly took up the stew, and began to eat it; she was in reality nearly starved.

"Now," said the Persian princess, when she had finished, "you had better do that mending, while I finish cooking and eat my own supper."

Dorothy obeyed. By the time the apron was neatly mended, the princess had finished cooking and eaten the pigeon. "Now, I wish to talk a little to you," said she. "I feel as if you deserved my confidence since you have penetrated my disguise. I am a Persian princess, as I said before, and I am travelling incognita to see the world and improve my mind, and also to rescue my brother, who is a Maltese prince and enchanted. My brother, when very young, went on his travels, was shipwrecked on the coast of Malta, and became a prince of that island. But he had enemies, and was enchanted. He is now a Maltese cat. I disguise myself as a cat in order to find him more readily. Now, for what do you most wish?"

Dorothy courtesied; she was really too impressed to speak.

"Answer," said the princess, imperiously.

"I—want," stammered Dorothy, "to — take my grandmother out of—the almshouse, and have her sit at the window in the sun in a cushioned chair and knit a silk stocking all day."

"Anything else?"

"I should like to—have her wear a bombazine gown and a—white lace cap with—lilac ribbons."

"You are a good girl," said the princess. "Now, listen. I see that you are not very pleasantly situated here, and I will teach you a way to escape. Take your hood off that peg over there, and come out with me. I want to find my portmanteau that I left under the hedge, a little way down the road."

Dorothy put on her hood and followed the princess down the road. The little girl could scarcely keep up with her; she seemed to fairly fly through the moonlight, trailing her gray robe after her.

"Here is my portmanteau," said the princess, when they had reached the hedge. The hedge was all white hawthorn and very sweet. The portmanteau had lain well under it. All Dorothy could see was a tiny leather wallet, that a cat could carry in her mouth. But the princess blew upon it three times, and suddenly a great leather trunk stood on the grass. The princess opened it, and Dorothy gave a little cry, her eyes were so dazzled. It was like a blaze of gold and silver and jewels. "Look at this," said the princess. And she took out of the trunk the splendid robe that was laid uppermost.

Dorothy looked; she could not say anything. The robe was woven of silk, with gold and silver threads, and embroidered with jewels.

"If you will give this to Dame Betsy for her eldest daughter's bridal dress, she will let you go," said the princess. She took a pair of silver shears out of the trunk and cut off a bit of the robe under a flounce. "Show that to Dame Betsy," said the princess, "and tell her you will give her the dress made of the same material, and she will let you go. Now you had better run home. I shall stay here and sleep under the hedge. I do not like Dame Betsy's house. Come here in the morning, when you have told her about the dress."

The princess sat down on the trunk, and it immediately shrunk into the little wallet; then she curled herself up on the grass under the flowery hedge. Dorothy ran home and crept noiselessly up to her bed in the garret.

In the morning, when the daughters came down to breakfast, they missed the cat. "Where is the cat?" they inquired indignantly of their mother. They suspected her of driving the cat away with the broom. They had quite a wrangle over it. Finally, the daughters all put on finery and went out shopping for some needles and pins; then Dorothy showed Dame Betsy the scrap of the splendid robe, and said to her what the princess had directed she should say.

Dame Betsy was very much surprised and disturbed. She did not wish to lose Dorothy, who was a great help to her; still, she had no doubt that a suitor would soon appear for her eldest daughter, if arrayed in so beautiful a bridal gown as that. She reflected how she might have a tea-party and invite all the neighbors, and display the robe, and how all the sons would come flocking to the door. Finally she consented, and Dorothy, as soon as her mistress's back was turned, ran out and away to the hedge, under which she knew the Persian princess to be concealed.

The princess looked up and rubbed her eyes. She had slept late, although the birds were singing loudly all around her. Dorothy courtesied and said that she had come for the robe. "Very well," replied the princess, "I will give it to you; then you must carry it and hang it over Dame Betsy's gate, and run back to me as fast as you are able."

Then the princess blew on the wallet until it became a trunk, and she took out the splendid robe and gave it to Dorothy, who carried it and hung it over Dame Betsy's gate just as she had been bidden. But as she was about to run away, she saw the little boy who lived next door peeping through his fence, so she stopped to bid him good-bye. He felt so sad that he wept, and Dorothy herself had tears in her eyes when she ran to join the princess.

Dorothy and the princess then set off on their travels; but nobody except Dorothy herself knew that there was a princess. Every one who met them saw simply a little girl and a beautiful gray cat. Finally they stopped at a pretty little village. "Here," said the princess, "we will rent a cottage."

They looked about until they found a charming cottage with a grape-vine over the door, and roses and marigolds in the yard; then Dorothy, at the princess's direction, went to the landlord and bargained for it.

Then they went to live in the cottage, and the princess taught Dorothy how to make lovely tidies and cushions and aprons out of the beautiful dresses in her trunk. She had a great store of them, but they were all made in the Persian fashion and were of no use in this country.

When Dorothy had made the pretty articles out of the rich dresses, she went out and sold them to wealthy ladies for high prices. She soon earned quite a sum of money, which she placed at interest in the bank, and she was then able to take her grandmother out of the almshouse. She bought a beautiful chair with a canary-colored velvet cushion, and she placed it at the window in the sun. She bought a bombazine dress and a white cap with lilac ribbons, and she had the silk stocking with the needles all ready.

But the day before the old grandmother came the princess bade Dorothy good-bye. "I am going out again on my travels," said she; "I wish to see more of the country, and I must continue my search for my brother, the Maltese prince."

So the princess kissed Dorothy, who wept; then she set forth on her travels. Dorothy gazed sorrowfully after her as she went. She saw a dainty little princess, trailing her gray velvets; but everybody else saw only a lovely gray cat hurrying down the road.

Dorothy's grandmother came to live with her. She sat in her cushioned chair, in the sunny window and knitted her silk stocking, and was a very happy old woman. Dorothy continued to make beautiful things out of the princess's dresses. It seemed as if there would never be any end to them. She had cut up many dresses, but there were apparently as many now as when she began. She saw no more of the princess, although she thought of her daily, until she was quite grown up and was a beautiful maiden with many suitors. Then, one day, she went to the city to deliver a beautiful cushion that she had made for some wealthy ladies, and there, in the drawing-room, she saw the Persian princess.

Dorothy was left in the room until the ladies came down, and as she sat there holding her cushion, she heard a little velvet rustle and a softly-hummed song in the Persian language. She looked, and there was the princess stepping across the floor, trailing her gray velvets.

"So you have come, dear Dorothy," said the princess.

Dorothy arose and courtesied, but the princess came close and kissed her. "What have you there?" she inquired.

Dorothy displayed the cushion; the princess laughed.

"It is quite a joke, is it not?" said she. "That cushion is for me to sleep on, and it is made out of one of my own dresses. The ladies have bought it for me. I have heard them talking about it. How do you fare, Dorothy, and how is your grandmother?"

Then Dorothy told the princess how the grandmother sat in the cushioned chair in the sunny window and knitted the silk stocking, and how she herself was to be married the next week to the little boy who had lived next door, but was now grown up and come a-wooing.

"Where is his grandmother?" asked the princess.

Dorothy replied that she was to live with them, and that there was already another cushioned chair in a sunny window, another bombazine dress and lace cap, and a silk stocking, in readiness, and that both grandmothers were to sit and knit in peace during the rest of their lives.

"Ah, well," said the princess, with a sigh, "if I were only back in Persia I would buy you a wedding present, but I do not know when that will be—the ladies are so kind."

Dorothy ventured to inquire if the princess had found her brother, the Maltese prince.

"Dear me, yes," replied the princess. "Why, he lives in this very house. He is out in the back parlor asleep on the sofa, this minute. Brother, dear brother, come here a second, I pray!"

With that a Maltese prince, with a long, aristocratic face, and beautiful, serious eyes, entered with a slow and stately tread. He was dressed in gray velvet, like his sister, and he wore white velvet mittens. Dorothy courtesied very low.

"Yes, I found my brother here, some time ago," said the princess; "but I have very little hope of freeing him from his enchantment. You see, there is only one thing that can break the spell: one of his mistresses must drive him out of the house with the broom, and I do not believe that either of them ever will—they are so exceedingly gracious and kind. I have tried to induce my brother to commit some little sin—to steal some cream or some meat, or to fly around the room as if he were in a fit (I myself have shown him how to do that), but he will not consent. He has too much dignity, and he is too fond of these ladies. And, if he should, I doubt if he would be driven out with the broom—they are so kind."

The princess sighed. The prince stood looking in a grave and stately manner at Dorothy, but he did not speak. "However," the princess continued, cheerfully, "we do very well here, and in some respects this is a more enlightened country than either Persia or Malta, and it is a privilege to live here. The ladies are very kind to us, and we are very fond of them; then, too, we see very fine company. And there are also Persian hangings and rugs which make it seem home-like. We are very well contented. I don't know, on the whole, that we are in any hurry to go away. But should either of the ladies ever take it into her head to drive my brother out of the house with the broom, we shall at once leave the country for Persia and Malta; for, after all, one's native land is dear."

The princess stopped talking, and began to hum her Persian song, and then the ladies entered the room. They greeted Dorothy kindly; then they began to call, "Vashti, Vashti, come here, pretty Vashti," and, "Muff, Muff, come here, pretty Muff." For they did not see the Persian princess and the Maltese prince, but two beautiful cats, whose names were Vashti and Muff.

"Just hear Vashti purr," said one of the ladies. "Come here, pretty Vashti, and try your new cushion."

And the ladies saw a cat sitting on the rich cushion, and another cat looking at her gravely, while Dorothy saw a Persian princess and a Maltese prince.

However, the ladies knew that there was something uncommon about their cats, and they sometimes suspected the truth themselves, but they thought it must be a fancy.

Dorothy left her cushion and went away, and that was the last time she ever saw the Persian princess. As she went out the door the princess pressed close to her. The ladies thought she mewed, but in reality she was talking.

"Good-bye, Dorothy," said she, "I hope you will live happily ever after. And as for my brother and I, we really enjoy ourselves; we are seeing the country and improving our minds, and we love the ladies. If one of them should drive him out with the broom, he will become a prince again, and we shall leave; but I do not know that it is desirable. A cat has a more peaceful life than a prince. Good-bye, dear Dorothy."

The princess was going closer to embrace Dorothy, but the ladies became alarmed; they thought that their beautiful cat was going to steal out of the house. So they called, and a maid with a white cap ran and caught the Persian princess, and carried her back to the drawing-room. The ladies thought she mewed as she was being carried in, but in reality she was calling back merrily, "Good-bye, and live happily ever after, dear Dorothy!"

WHERE THE CHRISTMAS-TREE GREW

It was afternoon recess at No. 4 District School, in Warner. There was a heavy snow-storm; so every one was in the warm school-room, except a few adventurous spirits who were tumbling about in the snow-drifts out in the yard, getting their clothes wet and preparing themselves for chidings at home. Their shrill cries and shouts of laughter floated into the school-room, but the small group near the stove did not heed them at all. There were five or six little girls and one boy. The girls, with the exception of Jenny Brown, were trim and sweet in their winter dresses and neat school-aprons; they perched on the desks and the arms of the settee with careless grace, like birds. Some of them had their arms linked. The one boy lounged against the blackboard. His dark, straight-profiled face was all aglow as he talked. His big brown eyes gazed now soberly and impressively at Jenny, then gave a gay dance in the direction of the other girls.

"Yes, it does—*honest!*" said he.

The other girls nudged one another softly; but Jenny Brown stood with her innocent, solemn eyes fixed upon Earl Munroe's face, drinking in every word.

"You ask anybody who knows," continued Earl; "ask Judge Barker, ask—the minister—"

"Oh!" cried the little girls; but the boy shook his head impatiently at them.

"Yes," said he; "you just go and ask Mr. Fisher to-morrow, and you'll see what he'll tell you. Why, look here"—Earl straightened himself and stretched out an arm like an orator—it's nothing more than *reasonable* that Christmas-trees grow wild with the presents all on 'em! What sense would there be in 'em if they didn't, I'd like to know? They grow in different places, of course; but these around here grow mostly on the mountain over there. They come up every spring, and they all blossom out about Christmas-time, and folks go hunting for them to give to the children. Father and Ben are over on the mountain to-day—"

"Oh, oh!" cried the little girls.

"I mean, I guess they are," amended Earl,

trying to put his feet on the boundary-line of truth. "I hope they'll find a full one."

Jenny Brown had a little, round, simple face; her thin brown hair was combed back and braided tightly in one tiny braid tied with a bit of shoe-string. She wore a nondescript gown, which nearly trailed behind, and showed in front her little, coarsely-shod feet, which toed-in helplessly. The gown was of a faded green color; it was scalloped and bound around the bottom, and had some green ribbon-bows down the front. It was, in fact, the discarded polonaise of a benevolent woman, who aided the poor substantially but not tastefully.

Jenny Brown was eight, and small for her age —a strange, gentle, ignorant little creature, never doubting the truth of what she was told, which sorely tempted the other children to impose upon her. Standing there in the school-room that stormy recess, in the midst of that group of wiser, richer, mostly older girls, and that one handsome, mischievous boy, she believed every word she heard.

This was her first term at school, and she had never before seen much of other children. She had lived her eight years all alone at home with her mother, and she had never been told about Christmas. Her mother had other things to think about. She was a dull, spiritless, reticent woman, who had lived through much trouble. She worked, doing washings and cleanings, like a poor feeble machine that still moves but has no interest in its motion. Sometimes the Browns had almost enough to eat, at other times they half starved. It was half-starving time just then; Jenny had not had enough to eat that day.

There was a pinched look on the little face upturned towards Earl Munroe's.

Earl's words gained authority by coming from himself. Jenny had always regarded him with awe and admiration. It was much that he should speak at all to her.

Earl Munroe was quite the king of this little district school. He was the son of the wealthiest man in town. No other boy was so well dressed, so gently bred, so luxuriously lodged and fed. Earl himself realized his importance, and had at times the loftiness of a young prince in his manner. Occasionally, some independent urchin would bristle with democratic spirit, and tell him to his face that he was "stuck up," and that he hadn't so much more to be proud of than other folks; that his grandfather wasn't anything but an old ragman!

Then Earl would wilt. Arrogance in a free country is likely to have an unstable foundation.

Earl tottered at the mention of his paternal grandfather, who had given the first impetus to the family fortune by driving a tin-cart about the country. Moreover, the boy was really pleasant and generous hearted, and had no mind, in the long run, for lonely state and disagreeable haughtiness. He enjoyed being lordly once in a while, that was all.

He did now, with Jenny—he eyed her with a gay condescension, which would have greatly amused his tin-peddler grandfather.

Soon the bell rung, and they all filed to their seats, and the lessons were begun.

After school was done that night, Earl stood in the door when Jenny passed out.

"Say, Jenny," he called, "when are you going over on the mountain to find the Christmas-tree? You'd better go pretty soon, or they'll be gone."

"That's so!" chimed in one of the girls. "You'd better go right off, Jenny."

She passed along, her face shyly dimpling with her little innocent smile, and said nothing. She would never talk much.

She had quite a long walk to her home. Presently, as she was pushing weakly through the new snow, Earl went flying past her in his father's sleigh, with the black horses and the fur-capped coachman. He never thought of asking her to ride. If he had, he would not have hesitated a second before doing so.

Jenny, as she waded along, could see the mountain always before her. This road led straight to it, then turned and wound around its base. It had stopped snowing, and the sun was setting clear. The great white mountain was all rosy. It stood opposite the red western sky. Jenny kept her eyes fixed upon the mountain. Down in the valley shadows her little simple face, pale and colorless, gathered another kind of radiance.

There was no school the next day, which was the one before Christmas. It was pleasant, and not very cold. Everybody was out; the little village stores were crowded; sleds trailing Christmas-greens went flying; people were hastening with parcels under their arms, their hands full.

Jenny Brown also was out. She was climbing Franklin Mountain. The snowy pine boughs bent so low that they brushed her head. She stepped deeply into the untrodden snow; the train of her green polonaise dipped into it, and swept it along. And all the time she was peering through those white fairy columns and arches for—a Christmas-tree.

That night, the mountain had turned rosy, and

faded, and the stars were coming out, when a frantic woman, panting, crying out now and then in her distress, went running down the road to the Munroe house. It was the only one between her own and the mountain. The woman rained some clattering knocks on the door—she could not stop for the bell. Then she burst into the house, and threw open the dining-room door, crying out in gasps:

"Hev you seen her? Oh, hev you? My Jenny's lost! She's lost! Oh, oh, oh! They said they saw her comin' up this way, this mornin'. *Hev* you seen her, *hev* you?"

Earl and his father and mother were having tea there in the handsome oak-panelled dining-room. Mr. Munroe rose at once, and went forward, Mrs. Munroe looked with a pale face around her silver tea-urn, and Earl sat as if frozen. He heard his father's soothing questions, and the mother's answers. She had been out at work all day; when she returned, Jenny was gone. Some one had seen her going up the road to the Munroes' that morning about ten o'clock. That was her only clew.

Earl sat there, and saw his mother draw the poor woman into the room and try to comfort her; he heard, with a vague understanding, his father order the horses to be harnessed immediately; he watched him putting on his coat and hat out in the hall.

When he heard the horses trot up the drive, he sprang to his feet. When Mr. Munroe opened the door, Earl, with his coat and cap on, was at his heels.

"Why, you can't go, Earl!" said his father, when he saw him. "Go back at once."

Earl was white and trembling. He half sobbed: "Oh, father, I must go!" said he.

"Earl, be reasonable. You want to help, don't you, and not hinder?" his mother called out of the dining-room.

Earl caught hold of his father's coat. "Father —look here—I—*I believe I know where she is!*"

Then his father faced sharply around, his mother and Jenny's stood listening in bewilderment, and Earl told his ridiculous, childish, and cruel little story. "I—didn't dream—she'd really be—such a little—goose as to—go," he choked out; "but she must have, for"—with brave candor—"I know she believed every word I told her."

It seemed a fantastic theory, yet a likely one. It would give method to the search, yet more alarm to the searchers. The mountain was a wide region in which to find one little child.

Jenny's mother screamed out, "Oh, if she's

lost on the mountain, they'll never find her! They never will, they never will! Oh, Jenny, Jenny, Jenny!"

Earl gave a despairing glance at her, and bolted up-stairs to his own room. His mother called pityingly after him; but he only sobbed back, "Don't, mother—please!" and kept on.

The boy, lying face downward on his bed, crying as if his heart would break, heard presently the church-bell clang out fast and furious. Then he heard loud voices down in the road, and the flurry of sleigh-bells. His father had raised the alarm, and the search was organized.

After a while Earl arose, and crept over to the window. It looked towards the mountain, which towered up, cold and white and relentless, like one of the ice-hearted giants of the old Indian tales. Earl shuddered as he looked at it. Presently he crawled down-stairs and into the parlor. In the bay-window stood, like a gay mockery, the Christmas-tree. It was a quite small one that year, only for the family—some expected guests had failed to come—but it was well laden. After tea the presents were to have been distributed. There were some for his father and mother, and some for the servants, but the bulk of them were for Earl.

By-and-by his mother, who had heard him

come down-stairs, peeped into the room, and saw him busily taking his presents from the tree. Her heart sank with sad displeasure and amazement. She would not have believed that her boy could be so utterly selfish as to think of Christmas-presents *then*.

But she said nothing. She stole away, and returned to poor Mrs. Brown, whom she was keeping with her; still she continued to think of it all that long, terrible night, when they sat there waiting, listening to the signal-horns over on the mountain.

Morning came at last and Mr. Munroe with it. No success so far. He drank some coffee and was off again. That was quite early. An hour or two later the breakfast-bell rang. Earl did not respond to it, so his mother went to the foot of the stairs and called him. There was a stern ring in her soft voice. All the time she had in mind his heartlessness and greediness over the presents. When Earl did not answer she went up-stairs, and found that he was not in his room. Then she looked in the parlor, and stood staring in bewilderment. Earl was not there, but neither were the Christmas-tree and his presents—they had vanished bodily!

Just at that moment Earl Munroe was hurrying down the road, and he was dragging his big sled, on which were loaded his Christmas-presents and the Christmas-tree. The top of the tree trailed in the snow, its branches spread over the sled on either side, and rustled. It was a heavy load, but Earl tugged manfully in an enthusiasm of remorse and atonement—a fantastic, extravagant atonement, planned by that same fertile fancy which had invented that story for poor little Jenny, but instigated by all the good, repentant impulses in the boy's nature.

On every one of those neat parcels, above his own name, was written in his big crooked, childish hand, "Jenny Brown, from—" Earl Munroe had not saved one Christmas-present for himself.

Pulling along, his eyes brilliant, his cheeks glowing, he met Maud Barker. She was Judge Barker's daughter, and the girl who had joined him in advising Jenny to hunt on the mountain for the Christmas-tree.

Maud stepped along, placing her trim little feet with dainty precision; she wore some new high-buttoned overshoes. She also carried a new beaver muff, but in one hand only. The other dangled mittenless at her side; it was pink with cold, but on its third finger sparkled a new gold ring with a blue stone in it.

"Oh, Earl!" she called out, "have they found Jenny Brown? I was going up to your house to — Why, Earl Munroe, what have you got there?"

"I'm carrying up my Cristmas-presents and the tree up to Jenny's—so she'll find 'em when she comes back," said the boy, flushing red. There was a little defiant choke in his voice.

"Why, what for?"

"I rather think they belong to her more'n they do to me, after what's happened."

"Does your mother know?"

"No; she wouldn't care. She'd think I was only doing what I ought."

"All of 'em?" queried Maud, feebly.

"You don't s'pose I'd keep any back?"

Maud stood staring. It was beyond her little philosophy.

Earl was passing on when a thought struck him.

"Say, Maud," he cried, eagerly, "haven't you something you can put in? Girls' things might please her better, you know. Some of mine are —rather queer, I'm afraid."

"What have you got?" demanded Maud.

"Well, some of the things are well enough. There's a lot of candy and oranges and figs and books; there's one by Jules Verne I guess she'll like; but there's a great big jack-knife, and—a brown velvet bicycle suit?"

"Why, Earl Munroe! what could she do with a bicycle suit?"

"I thought, maybe, she could rip the seams to 'em, an' sew 'em some way, an' get a basque cut, or something. Don't you s'pose she could?" Earl asked, anxiously.

"I don't know; her mother could tell," said Maud.

"Well, I'll hang it on, anyhow. Maud, haven't you anything to give her?"

"I—don't know."

Earl eyed her sharply. "Isn't that muff new?"

"Yes."

"And that ring?"

Maud nodded. "She'd be delighted with 'em. Oh, Maud, put 'em in!"

Maud looked at him. Her pretty mouth quivered a little; some tears twinkled in her blue eyes.

"I don't believe my mother would let me," faltered she. "You—come with me, and I'll ask her."

"All right," said Earl, with a tug at his sled-rope.

He waited with his load in front of Maud's house until she came forth radiant, lugging a big basket. She had her last winter's red cashmere dress, a hood, some mittens, cake and biscuit, and nice slices of cold meat.

"Mother said these would be much more *suitable* for her," said Maud, with a funny little imitation of her mother's manner.

Over across the street another girl stood at the gate, waiting for news.

"Have they found her?" she cried. "Where are you going with all those things?"

Somehow, Earl's generous, romantic impulse spread like an epidemic. This little girl soon came flying out with her contribution; then there were more—quite a little procession filed finally down the road to Jenny Brown's house.

The terrible possibilities of the case never occurred to them. The idea never entered their heads that little, innocent, trustful Jenny might never come home to see that Christmas-tree which they set up in her poor home.

It was with no surprise whatever that they saw, about noon, Mr. Munroe's sleigh, containing Jenny and her mother and Mrs. Munroe, drive up to the door.

Afterwards they heard how a wood-cutter had found Jenny crying, over on the east side of the mountain, at sunset, and had taken her home with him. He lived five miles from the village, and was an old man, not able to walk so far that night to tell them of her safety. His wife had been very good to the child. About eleven o'clock some of the searchers had met the old man plodding along the mountain-road with the news.

They did not stop for this now. They shouted to Jenny to "come in, quick!" They pulled her with soft violence into the room where they had been at work. Then the child stood with her hands clasped, staring at the Christmas-tree. All too far away had she been searching for it. The Christmas-tree grew not on the wild mountain-side, in the lonely woods, but at home, close to warm, loving hearts; and that was where she found it.

WHERE SARAH JANE'S DOLL WENT

In the first place, Sarah Jane had no right to take the doll to school, but the temptation was too much for her. The doll was new—it was, in fact, only one day old—and such a doll! Rag, of course—Sarah Jane had heard only vague rumors of other kinds—but no more like the ordinary rag doll than a fairy princess is like a dairymaid. The minute that Sarah Jane saw it she knew at once that there never had been such a doll. It was small—not more than seven or eight inches tall—not by any means the usual big, sprawling, moon-faced rag baby with its arms standing out at right angles with its body. It was tiny and genteel in figure, slim-waisted, and straight-backed. It was made of, not common cotton cloth, but linen—real glossy white linen—which Sarah Jane's mother, and consequently the doll's grandmother, had spun and wove. Its face was colored after a fashion which was real high art to Sarah Jane. The little cheeks and mouth were sparingly flushed with cranberry juice, and the eyes beamed blue with indigo. The nose was delicately traced with a quill dipped in its grandfather's ink-stand, and though not quite as natural as the rest of the features, showed fine effort. Its little wig was made from the fine ravellings of Serena's brown silk stockings.

Serena was Sarah Jane's married sister, who lived in the next house across the broad green yard, and she had made this wonderful doll. She brought it over one evening just before Sarah Jane went to bed. "There," said she, "if you'll be a real good girl I'll give you this."

"Oh!" cried Sarah Jane, and she could say no more.

Serena, who was only a girl herself, dandled the doll impressively before her bewildered eyes. It was dressed in a charming frock made from a bit of Serena's best French calico. The frock was of a pale lilac color with roses sprinkled over it, and was cut with a low neck and short puffed sleeves.

"Now, Sarah Jane," said Serena, admonishingly, "there's one thing I want to tell you: you mustn't carry this doll to school. If you do, you'll lose it; and if you do, you won't get an-

other very soon. It was a good deal of work to
make it. Now you mind what I say."

"Yes, ma'am," said Sarah Jane. It was not
her habit to say ma'am to her sister Serena, if
she was twelve years older than she; but she
did now, and reached out impatiently for the
doll.

"Well, you remember," said Serena. "If you
take it to school and lose it, it 'll be the last doll
you'll get."

And Sarah Jane said, "Yes, ma'am," again.

She had to go to bed directly, but she took
the new doll with her; that was not forbidden,
much to her relief. And before she went to
sleep she had named her with a most flowery
name, nothing less than Lily Rosalie Violet May.
It took her a long time to decide upon it, but
she was finally quite satisfied, and went to sleep
hugging Lily Rosalie, and dreamed about her
next day's spelling lesson—that she failed and
went to the foot of the class.

It was singular, but for once a dream of Sarah
Jane's came true. She actually did miss in her
spelling lesson the next day; and although she
did not go quite to the foot of the class, she went
very near to it. But if Sarah Jane was not able
to spell *scissors* correctly, she could have spelled
with great success Lily Rosalie Violet May. All

the evening she had been printing it over and over on a fly-leaf of her spelling-book. She could feel no interest in scissors, which had no connection, except a past one, with her beloved new doll.

Poor Sarah Jane lived such a long way from school that she had to carry her dinner with her, so there was a whole day's separation, when she had only possessed Lily Rosalie for a matter of twelve hours. It was hard.

She told some of her particular cronies about her, and described her charms with enthusiasm, but it was not quite equal to displaying her in person.

The little girls promised to come over and see the new doll just as soon as their mothers would let them, and one, Ruth Gurney, who was Sarah Jane's especial friend, said she would go home with her that very night—she didn't believe her mother would care—but they were going to have company at tea, and she was afraid if she were late, and had to sit at the second table, that she wouldn't get any currant tarts.

Sarah Jane did not urge her; she had a shy little pride of her own; but she felt deeply hurt that Ruth could prefer currant tarts to a sight of Lily Rosalie.

She was rather apt to loiter on her way home.

There was much temptation to at this time of the year, when the meadows on either side of the road were so brimful of grass and flowers, when the air was so sweet, and so many birds were singing. There was a brook on the way, and occasionally Sarah Jane used to stop and have a little secret wade. It was one of those pleasures which, although not actually prohibited, was doubtful. Sarah Jane had at times got the hem of her little blue calico gown draggled, and met with a reprimand at home.

But to-night neither nodding way-side flowers nor softly rippling brook had any attraction for her. Straight home, her little starched white sun-bonnet pointing ahead unswervingly, her small pattering feet never turning aside from the narrow beaten track between the way-side grasses, she went to Lily Rosalie Violet May.

She found her just as beautiful as when she left her. That long day of absence, filled in with her extravagant childish fancy, had not caused her charms to lessen in the least.

Sarah Jane ran straight to the linen chest, in whose till she had hidden for safety the precious doll, and there she lay, her indigo blue eyes staring up, smiling at her with the sweet cranberry-colored smile which Serena had fixed on her face. Sarah Jane caught her up in rapture.

Her mother told Serena that night that she didn't know when she'd seen the child so tickled with anything as she was with that doll.

"She didn't carry it to the school, did she?" said Serena.

"No. I guess she won't want to, as long as you told her not to," replied her mother.

Sarah Jane had been always an obedient little girl; but—she had never before had Lily Rosalie Violet May. Her mother did not consider that.

Sarah Jane did not have a pocket made in her dress; it was not then the fashion. Instead, she wore a very large-sized one, made of stout cotton, tied around her waist by a string under her dress skirt. The next day, when Sarah Jane went to school, she carried in this pocket her new doll. She was quite late this morning, so there was no time to display it before school commenced.

Once, when the high arithmetic class was out on the floor, she pulled it slyly out of her pocket, held it under her desk, and poked Ruth Gurney, who sat in the next seat.

"Oh!" gasped Ruth, almost aloud. The doll seemed to fascinate everybody. "Let me take it," motioned Ruth; but Sarah Jane shook a wise head, and slid Lily Rosalie back in her pocket. She was not going to run the risk of having her confiscated by the teacher. But when recess came Sarah Jane was soon the proud little centre of an admiring group.

"Sarah Jane's got the handsomest new doll," one whispered to another, and they all crowded around. Even some of the "big girls" came, and two or three of the big boys. Sarah Jane was one of the smallest girls in school, and sat in the very front seat. Now she felt like a big girl herself. This wonderful doll raised her at once to a position of importance. There she stood in the corner by the window, and proudly held it. She wore a blue cotton dress cut after the fashion of Lily Rosalie's, with a low neck and short sleeves, displaying her dimpled childish neck and arms. Her round cheeks were flushed with a softer pink than the doll's, and her honest brown eyes were full of delight.

One and another of the girls begged for the privilege of taking the doll a moment for a closer scrutiny, and Sarah Jane would grant it, and then watch them with thinly veiled anxiety. Suppose their fingers shouldn't be quite clean, and there should be a spot on Lily Rosalie's beautiful white linen skin! One of the girls rubbed her cheeks to see if the red would come off, and Sarah Jane wriggled.

Joe West was one of the big boys who had joined the group. Years after, he was Joseph B. West, an eminent city lawyer. Years after that, he was Judge West of the Superior Court. Now he was simply Joe West, a tall, lanky boy with a long rosy face and a high forehead. His arms came too far through his jacket sleeves, and showed his wrists, which looked unnaturally knobby and bony. He went barefoot all summer long, and was much given to chewing sassafras.

He offered a piece to Sarah Jane now, extracting it with gravity from a mass of chalk, top strings, buttons, nails, and other wealth with which his pocket was filled.

Sarah Jane accepted it with a modest little blush, and plumped it into her rosy mouth.

Then Joe West followed up his advantage. "Say, Sarah Jane," said he, "lemme take her a minute."

She eyed him doubtfully. Somehow she mistrusted him. Joe West had rather the reputation of being a wag and a sore tease.

"She's just the prettiest doll I ever saw," Joe went on. "Lemme take her just a minute, Sarah Jane; now do."

"He's just stuffing you, Sarah Jane; don't you let him touch it," spoke out one of the big girls.

"Stufling" was a very expressive word in the language of the school. Sarah Jane shook her head with a timid little smile, and hugged Lily Rosalie tighter.

"Now do, Sarah Jane. I wouldn't be stingy. Haven't I just given you some sassafras?"

That softened her a little. The spicy twang of the sassafras was yet on her tongue. "I'm afraid you won't give her back to me," murmured she.

"Yes, I will, honest. Now do, Sarah Jane."

It was against her better judgment; the big girl again raised her warning voice; but Joe West adroitly administered a little more flattery, and followed it up with entreaty, and Sarah Jane, yielding, finally put her precious little white linen baby into his big grimy, out-reaching hands.

"Oh, the pretty little sing!" said Joe West then, in an absurdly soft voice, and dandled it up and down. "What's its name, Sarah Jane?"

And Sarah Jane in her honesty and simplicity repeated that flowery name.

"Lily Rosalie Violet May," said Joe, after her, softly. And everybody giggled.

A pink color spread all over Sarah Jane's face and dimpled neck; tears sprang to her eyes. She felt as if they were poking fun at something sacred; her honest childish confidence was be-

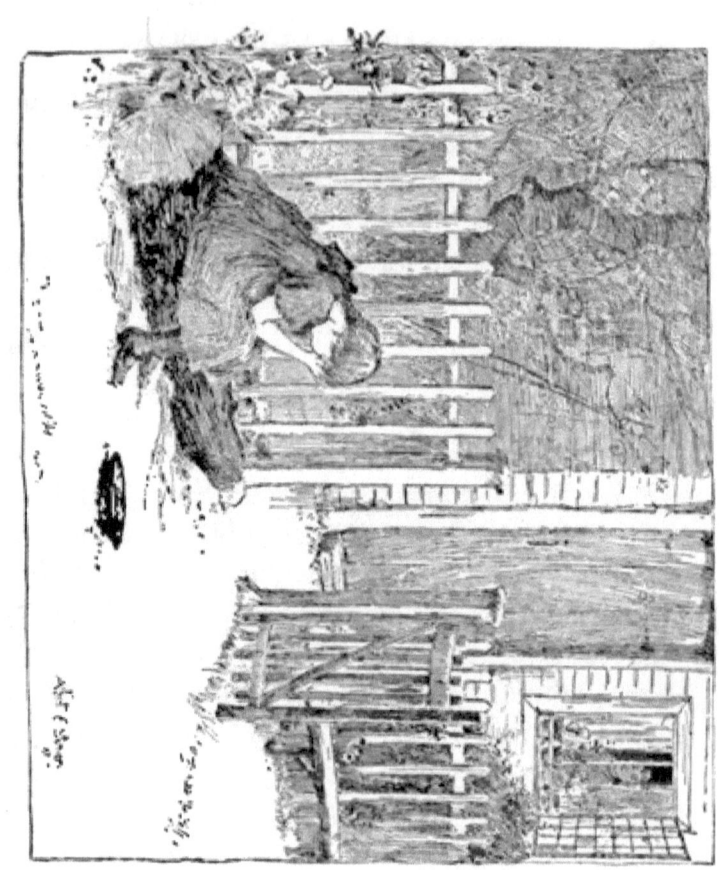

"SARAH JANE SAT DOWN BESIDE THE ROAD AND WEPT"

trayed. "Give her back to me, Joe West!" she cried.

But Joe only dandled it out of her reach, and then the bell rang. The children trooped back into the school-room, and Joe quietly slipped the doll into his pocket and marched gravely to his seat.

Every time when Sarah Jane gazed around at him he was studying his geography with the most tireless industry. She could hardly wait for school to be done; when it was, she tried to get to Joe, but he was too quick for her. He had started with his long stride down the road before she could get to the door. She called after him, but he appeared to have suddenly grown deaf. The other girls condoled with her, all but the big girl who had given the warning. "You'd ought to have listened to me," said she, severely, as she tied on her sun-bonnet in the entry. "I told you how it would be, letting a boy have hold of it."

Sarah Jane was not much comforted. She crept forlornly along towards home. Joe West's house was on the way. There was a field south of it. As she came to this field she saw Joe out there with the bossy. This bossy, which was tethered to an old apple-tree, was cream-colored, with a white star on her forehead and a neck and head like a deer. She stood knee-deep in the daisies and clover, and looked like a regular picture-calf. If Sarah Jane had not been so much occupied with her own troubles, she would have stopped to gaze with pleasure at the pretty creature.

Joe stood at her head and appeared to be teasing her. She twitched away from him, and lunged at him playfully with her budding horns.

"Joe! Joe!" called quaking little Sarah Jane.

Joe West gave one glance at her; his face flushed a burning red; then he left the bossy and went with long strides across the fields towards his home. The poor girl followed him.

"Joe! Joe!" called the little despairing voice, but he never turned his head.

Sarah Jane got past his house; then she sat down beside the road and wept. She did not know how Joe West, remorseful and penitent, was peeping at her from his window. She did not know of the tragedy which had just been enacted over there in the clover-field. The bossy calf, who was hungry for all strange articles of food, had poked her inquiring nose into Joe West's jacket pocket, whence a bit of French calico emerged, had caught hold of it, and, in short, had then and there eaten up Lily Rosalie Violet May. Joe had made an attempt to pull her by her silken wig out of that greedy mouth, but the bossy calmly chewed on.

It was just as well that Sarah Jane did not know it at the time. She had enough to bear—her own distress over the loss of the doll, and the reproaches of Serena and her mother. They agreed that the loss of the doll served her right for her disobedience, and that nothing should be said to Joe West. They also thought the affair too trivial to fuss over. Lily Rosalie even in her designer's eyes was not what she was to Sarah Jane.

"If you'd minded me you wouldn't have lost it," said Serena. "I am not going to make you another."

Sarah Jane hung her head meekly. But in the course of three months she had another doll in a very unexpected and curious way.

One evening there was a knock on the side door, and when it was opened there was no one there, but on the step lay a big package directed to Sarah Jane. It contained a real bought doll, with a china head and a cloth body, who was gorgeously and airily attired in pink tarlatan with silver spangles. The memory of Lily Rosalie paled.

There was great wonder and speculation. Nobody dreamed how poor Joe West had driven cows from pasture, and milked, and chopped wood, out of school-hours, and taken every cent he had earned and bought this doll to atone for the theft of Lily Rosalie Violet May.

Sarah Jane's mother declared that she should not carry this doll, no matter whence it came, to school, and she never did but once—that was on her birthday, and she teased so hard, and promised not to let any one take her, that her mother consented.

At recess Sarah Jane was again the centre of attraction. She turned that wonderful pink tarlatan lady round and round before the admiring eyes; but when Joe West, meek and mildly conciliatory, approached the circle, she clutched her tightly and turned her back on him.

"I'm not going to have Joe West steal another doll," said she. And Joe colored and retreated.

Years afterwards, when Joe was practising law in the city, and came home for a visit, and Sarah Jane was so grown-up that she wore a white muslin hat with rosebuds, and a black silk mantilla, to church, she knew the whole story, and they had a laugh over it.

SEVENTOES' GHOST

"You needn't waste any more time talkin' about it, Benjamin; you can jest take that puppy-dog and carry him off. I don't care what you do with him; you can carry him back where you got him, or give him away, or swap him off; but jest as sure as you leave him here half an hour longer, I'll call Jimmy up from the hay-field and have him shoot him. I won't have a dog round the place, nohow. Couldn't keep Seventoes a minute; he's dreadful scart of dogs."

"Grandsir—"

"Take that puppy-dog and go along, I tell ye. I won't have any more talk about it."

Benjamin Wellman, small and slight, sandy-haired and blue-eyed, stood before his grandfather, who sat in his big arm-chair in the east door. Benjamin held in his right hand an old rope, which was attached to a leather strap around a puppy's neck. The puppy pulled at the rope, keeping it taut all the time. He also yelped shrilly. He did not like to be tied. The puppy was not a pretty one, being yellow and very clumsy; but Benjamin thought him a beauty. He had urged to his grandfather that there would not be a dog to equal him in the neighborhood when he was grown up, but the old man had not been moved.

There were tears in Benjamin's pretty blue eyes, but his square chin looked squarer. He tried to speak again. "Grandsir—" he began.

"Not another word," said his grandfather.

Benjamin looked past his grandfather into the kitchen. His mother sat in there stemming currants. He went around to the other door and entered, dragging the puppy after him.

"Mother," he said, in a low voice, "can't I keep him?"

His grandfather in the east door looked around suspiciously, but he could hear nothing; he was somewhat deaf.

"No; not if your grandfather don't want you to," said his mother; "you know I can't let you, Benjamin."

The puppy was whining piteously, and Benjamin seemed to echo it when he spoke. "I don't see why he don't want me to. It ain't as if Cæsar was a common puppy. You ask him, mother."

"No," returned his mother; "it won't do any good. You know how much he thinks of Seventoes, and the dog might kill him when he was grown."

"Wouldn't care if he did," muttered Benjamin; "nothing but a cross old stealing cat; don't begin to be worth what this puppy is."

"Now, Benjamin, you mustn't talk any more about it," said his mother, severely. "Grandsir does too much for you and me for you to make any fuss about a thing like this. Take that puppy and run right along with it, as he tells you to."

Grandsir's suspicions suddenly took shape then. "Benjamin, you run right along," he called out; "don't stand there teasing your mother about it."

So Benjamin gathered the puppy up into his arms with a jerk—it was impossible to lead him any distance—and plunged out of the house. He gave two or three little choking sobs as he hurried along. It was a hot day, and he was tired and disappointed and discouraged. He had walked three miles over to the village and back to get that puppy, and now he had to walk a mile more to give it away. He had no doubt whatever as to the disposal of it; he knew Sammy Tucker would give it a hearty welcome, for there was an understanding to that effect. Benjamin had been a little doubtful as to the reception the puppy might have from his grandfather; but when Mr. Dyer, who kept the village grocery store, had offered it to him three weeks before, he had not had the courage to refuse. Sammy Tucker, too, had been in the store, buying three bars of soap for his mother, and he had looked on admiringly and enviously. When Benjamin had mentioned hesitatingly his doubts about his grandfather, Sammy had pricked up his ears.

"Say, Ben, you give him to me if your grandfather won't let you keep him," he had whispered, with a nudge. "Father said I might have a dog soon as there was a good chance, and Mr. Dyer won't want it back. He's giv away all but this, and he wants to get rid of 'em. They're common kind of dogs, anyhow. I heard him say so."

Benjamin had looked at him stiffly. "Oh, I guess grandsir 'll let me keep this puppy, he's such a smart one," he had answered, with dignity.

"Well, you ask him, and if he won't, I'll take him," said Sammy.

But Benjamin had not asked his grandfather. He had not had courage to run the risk. He had waited the three weeks which the storekeeper had said must elapse before the little dog could leave its mother, and then had gone over to the village and brought it home, without a word to any one, trusting to the puppy's own attractions to plead for it. It had seemed to Benjamin that nobody could resist that puppy. But Grandfather Wellman had all his life preferred cats to dogs, and now he was childishly fond of Seventoes. Benjamin's mother often said that she didn't know what grandsir would do if anything happened to Seventoes.

Benjamin, going out of the yard with the puppy under his arm, could see Seventoes sitting on the shed roof. That and the ledge of the old well behind the barn were his favorite perches. Grandfather Wellman thought he chose them because he was so afraid of dogs. Benjamin looked at him, and wished Cæsar was big enough to shake him. He had named the puppy Cæsar on his way home from the village. There was a great mastiff over there by the same name. Benjamin had always admired this big Cæsar, and now thought he would name his dog after him. It was the same principle reduced on which Benjamin himself had been named after Benjamin Franklin.

Benjamin trudged down the road, kicking up the dust with his toes. That was something he had been told not to do, so now in this state of mind he liked to do it. The sun beat down fiercely upon his small red cropped head in the burned straw-hat, and his slender shoulders in the calico blouse. The puppy was large and fat for his age, and made his arms ache. The stone-walls on both sides of the road were hidden with wild-rose and meadowsweet bushes; the fields were dotted with hay-makers; now and then a loaded hay-cart loomed up in the road. Many boys no older than Benjamin had to work hard in the hay-fields, but Grandfather Wellman was too careful of him; he would not let him work much in vacation; he had never been considered very strong. But Benjamin did not think of that. One grievance will outweigh a hundred benefits. He hugged the struggling puppy tight in his arms and trudged on painfully, brooding over his wrongs.

He muttered to himself as he went, "Wanted a dog ever since I was born. All the other boys have got 'em. 'Ain't never had nothing but an old cat. Sha'n't never have a chance to get such a dog as this again. Wish something would happen to that old cat; shouldn't care a mite." He stubbed more fiercely into the dust, and it flew higher; a squirrel ran across the road, and he looked at it with an indifferent scowl.

When he reached Sammy Tucker's house he saw Sammy out in the great north yard raking hay with his father. Sammy looked up and saw Benjamin coming.

"Holloa!" he sang out, eagerly. Then he dropped his rake and raced into the road. His black eyes winked fast with excitement. "Say, won't he let you keep him, Ben?" he cried.

"No; he won't let me keep nothing."

"Going to let me have him, then?"

"S'pose so."

Sammy reached forth his eager hands, and took the kicking puppy from Benjamin's reluctant arms. "Nice fellar—nice little fellar," said he, tenderly.

"I've named him Cæsar," said Benjamin.

"That's a good name," assented Sammy. "Hi, Cæsar! Hi, sir!"

Sammy's father came smilingly forward to the fence; he was fond of dogs. He also took the puppy, and talked to it. Benjamin thought to himself that he wished his grandfather was more like Sammy's father. He looked on gloomily.

"Hate to give it up, don't you, Ben?" said Mr. Tucker, kindly.

"Sha'n't never have such a chance again."

"Oh yes, you will; your grandfather 'll let you have a dog some time."

"No; he won't never let me have nothing."

"Oh, don't you give up yet, Ben."

Benjamin shook his head like a discouraged old man, and turned to go home.

"Sammy 'll feed him, and take real good care of him, and you can come over here and see him," Mr. Tucker called after him, as he went down the road.

Benjamin thought to himself that he should not want to, as he marched wearily homeward. His arms were lightened of the puppy, but his heart seemed heavy within him. Two boys whom he knew sang out to him from a load of hay, but he gave only a grim nod in response. "*They've* got a dog," he muttered; and indeed the pretty shepherd dog was following after the load.

Benjamin, when he came in sight of home, thought he would take a short-cut through the orchard. He meditated stealing up the back stairs to his chamber, staying up there, and saying that he did not want any supper; he was not hungry. They had not cut the grass in the orchard, and he plunged through clover, feathery grass, and daisies to his waist. He felt pleased to think how he was making a furrow through his grandfather's hay. He emerged from the orchard, and went on towards the barn; directly back of it was the old well. When he reached that he stopped short. There was Seventoes—beautiful great yellow cat—stretched in the sun, all his wonderful seven-toed paws spread out. The ledge of the old well was a strange place for a cat, but Seventoes was fond of it, and stayed there much of the time when he was not on the shed roof.

Benjamin walked close to the well and looked at Seventoes. His small face was burning red with the heat; his blue eyes gleamed angrily. "You lazy old cat," said he. He stood a second longer; then he thrust out his right hand and gave Seventoes a push. There was a piteous yawl and a great clawing, and Seventoes was out of sight. Benjamin ran. He gasped; a white streak was settling around his mouth. He was well versed in Bible stories, and he thought of Cain. What had he done? What would happen to him? Could he ever get away from his guilt, run fast as he would? Benjamin ran as he had never run before, his heart pounding, although he did not know clearly what he was running for. He tore around the barn, through the pasture bars, towards the house. When he came in sight of the shed a great qualm of guilt and remorse forced him to glance up at the place where poor Seventoes had so loved to sit, and where he would sit no more. Benjamin glanced, then he stood stock-still, fairly aghast with awe and terror—*there sat Seventoes!*

All the red faded out of Benjamin's cheeks. He had never been encouraged in superstitious beliefs, but he was an imaginative child, and just now bewildered and unstrung. He stared at the shed roof. Yes! he saw Seventoes there, and Seventoes was at the bottom of the old well. Had he not seen him fall, clawing, down?

Benjamin rushed staggering into the kitchen. "Oh, grandsir! oh, mother!" he wailed—"oh, I've pushed Seventoes into the old well and drowned him, and his ghost's sitting on the shed roof! Oh, mother!"

Grandfather Wellman was confined to his chair with rheumatism, but he arose. "Pushed Seventoes into the well," he repeated, while Benjamin's mother turned as pale as her son.

"I have—I have," sobbed Benjamin. "I didn't know I was going to, but I have. And he's in the well, and he's sitting on the shed roof too. Oh!"

"What do you mean?" his mother gasped. "Stop acting so, and tell me what you've done."

"I pushed Seventoes into the old well. I didn't know I was going to, but I did; and he's dead in there, and he's on the shed roof. Oh, mother!"

"You 'ain't pushed that cat into the well?" groaned Grandfather Wellman. "If you have—" He was trying to limp across the kitchen with his cane. He, too, was pale, and trembling from head to foot. "Hannah," he said to Benjamin's mother, "you come right along quick, and see if we can't get him out. I wouldn't take a hundred dollars for that cat."

Benjamin's mother started. Benjamin, sobbing and trembling, was clinging to her. Just then *Seventoes walked in through the east door*, his splendid ringed tail waving a little uneasily, but not a hair of him was hurt. A frightened cat can run faster than a guilty little boy, and Seventoes had found his unusual number of claws of good service in climbing a well and retarding his progress towards the bottom.

They all looked.

"Is it—Seventoes?" gasped Benjamin, with wild eyes.

"Of course it's Seventoes," growled his grandfather. "I'd like to know what you've been cutting up so for. Pussy, pussy, pussy."

Benjamin's mother took him over to the sink, and put some water on his head, and made him drink some. "There's no such thing as a ghost, and you're acting very silly," said she; "but I don't wonder you are scared, when you've done such a dreadful thing. It scares me to think of it. It was 'most as bad as killing somebody. I never thought a boy of mine would do such a thing. Grandsir good as he is to you, too."

"I—won't ever do so—again," sobbed Benjamin, all trembling. "I'm sorry; I *am* sorry."

Benjamin was not whipped, the scourging of his own conscience had been severe enough, but he sat pale and sober in the kitchen, while grandsir, with Seventoes on his knees, and his mother talked to him.

"If you ever do anything like this again, Benjamin," said his grandfather, "I shall be ha'sh with you, ha'sher than I've ever been, and you must remember it."

"I guess he must," said his mother. "It was a dreadful wicked thing, and he should be punished now if I didn't think he'd suffered enough from his own guilty conscience for this time, and would never as long as he lived do such a terrible thing again."

"I won't—I—won't!" choked Benjamin.

At supper-time, when the new milk was brought in from the barn, Benjamin filled a saucer with it and carried it to the door for Seventoes. He filled it so full that he spilled it all the way over the clean kitchen floor, but his mother said nothing. Seventoes lapped his milk happily; Benjamin, with his little contrite, tear-stained face, stood watching him, and grandsir sat in his arm-chair. Over in the fields the haymakers were pitching the last loads into the carts; the east sky was red with the reflected color of the west. Everything was sweet and cool and peaceful, and the sun was not going down on Benjamin's childish wrath. His grandfather put out his hand and patted his little red cropped head, "You're always going to be a good boy after this, ain't you, sonny?"

"Yes, sir," said Benjamin, and he got down on his knees and hugged Seventoes.

LITTLE MIRANDY
AND HOW SHE EARNED HER SHOES

By the 1st of June Mrs. Thayer had the sun-bonnets done. There were four of them, for the four youngest girls—Eliza, Mary Ann, Harriet, and Mirandy. She had five daughters besides these, but two were married and gone away from home, and the other three were old enough to make their own sun-bonnets.

There were four Thayer boys; one of them came next to Mirandy, the youngest girl, the others ranked upward in age from Harriet, who was eleven, to Sarah Jane, who was sixteen. There were thirteen sons and daughters in all in Josiah Thayer's family, and eleven were at home. It was hard work to get enough from the stony New England farm to feed them; and let Mrs. Thayer card and spin and dye and weave as she would, the clothing often ran short. And so it happened that little Mirandy Thayer, aged six, had no shoes to her feet.

One Sunday in June she cried because she had to go to meeting barefooted.

"Ain't you ashamed of yourself, a great big girl like you, crying?" said her mother, sternly. "You go right over there, and sit down on the settle till father gets hitched up, and Daniel, you go and sit down 'side of her, and teach her the first question in the catechism. She'd ought to find out there's something else to be thought about on the Sabbath day besides shoes."

So Mirandy, sniffing between the solemn words, repeated them after Daniel, who was twelve years old, and knew his catechism quite thoroughly. And when the great farm wagon, with the team of oxen, stood before the door, she climbed in with the rest without a murmur.

But sitting in the meeting-house through the two hours' discourse, she drew up her little bare feet under her blue petticoat, and going down the aisle afterwards, she crouched, making it sweep the floor, until her mother dragged her up forcibly by one arm.

"Ain't you ashamed of yourself?" she whispered. "A great big girl like you!"

Mirandy was in reality very small for her age, and everybody called her "little;" but she got very few privileges on account of her youth and littleness. In those days, and especially in a family like Josiah Thayer's, where there were so many children that each had to scratch for itself at an early age or go without, six years was considered comparatively mature, and the child who had lived that long was not exempt from many duties.

So Mrs. Thayer did not think herself in the least severe when she said to Mirandy after meeting: "If you want some shoes so bad, you'll have to work an' earn 'em."

Mirandy looked up inquiringly at her mother.

"You can pick berries an' sell 'em," replied her mother. "You're plenty big enough to."

Mirandy said nothing, and soon her mother set her to rocking Jonathan in his red wooden cradle; but as she sat, with her small bare foot on the rocker, ambition expanded wider and wider in her childish soul, and she resolved that she would earn some shoes.

The berries were not ripe before the middle of July. She had some five weeks to wait before she could fairly begin work. But not a day passed that she did not visit the pastures to see if the berries were ripe. She brought home so many partially ripe ones for samples that her brothers and sisters remonstrated. They, too, were vitally interested in the berry crop in behalf of shoes and many other things. "She won't leave any berries on the bushes to get ripe if she picks so many green ones," they complained, and her mother issued a stern decree that Mirandy should not go to the berry pasture until the berries were fairly ripe.

But at last, one hot morning in July, the squad of berry-pickers started. There were four Thayer girls and two Thayer boys, besides Jonathan, the baby, whom Eliza dragged in his little wooden wagon.

"If you go berrying this mornin', you've got to take Jonathan with you," Mrs. Thayer had said. "Dorcas is weaving, an' Lyddy an' I have got to dye. You'll have to take him out in the pasture with you, an' tend him."

The berry pasture whither they were bound was about a half-mile from home. The two boys scurried on ahead, the four yellow sun-bonnets marched bravely on, and Jonathan's wagon rattled behind.

"The berries are real thick," said Harriet; "but they say the bushes are loaded with 'em over in Cap'n Moseby's lot, an' they're as big as walnuts."

"He can't use quarter of 'em himself," returned Mary Ann. "I call it real stingy not to let folks go in there pickin'!" She nodded her sun-bonnet indignantly.

When they reached the berry pasture, they fell to work eagerly. Jonathan's wagon was drawn up on one side, under the shade of a pine-tree, and Mirandy was bidden to have an eye to him. Nobody had much faith in the seriousness of Mirandy's picking, and they thought that she might as well tend Jonathan and leave them free.

But Mirandy stationed herself at a bush near Jonathan, and began with a will. They all had birch baskets fastened at their waists to pick into, and they had brought buckets to fill. Mirandy had hers as well as the rest.

The yellow sun-bonnets and the palm-leaf hats waved about among the bushes, and the berries fell fast into the birch-bark baskets. Mirandy stayed close to Jonathan, as she had been bidden, and she struggled bravely with her berry bush, but it was too tall for her; the bushes in this pasture were very tall. Mirandy tugged the branches down, and panted for breath. She was eager to fill her basket as soon as anybody. She heard Harriet and Mary Ann talking near her, although she could not see them.

"Cap'n Moseby's pasture is right over there. You get over the stone-wall, and go across one field, and you come to it," remarked Harriet.

"I s'pose the berries are as thick as spatters," said Mary Ann, with a sigh.

"Dan'l says the bushes are dragging down with 'em."

"Well," said Mary Ann, "nobody would dare to go there, for he keeps that great black dog, and I've heard he watches with a gun."

"So've I. No; I shouldn't dare to go. I s'pose it would be stealing, anyway."

"I don't s'pose 'twould," rejoined Harriet, hotly. "I guess if anything is free, berry pastures are. Who planted berry bushes, I'd like to know?"

"I s'pose the Lord did," said Mary Ann. "Mebbe it ain't stealin', but anyhow I shouldn't dare to go there."

"I shouldn't," agreed Harriet; "an' I know Dan'l and Abijah wouldn't."

Mirandy listened; she thought both Harriet and Mary Ann very wise. She trusted to their conclusion that it would not be stealing to pick Cap'n Moseby's berries, but she privately thought she would "dare to."

Mirandy did not know what fear was; dogs did not alarm her in the least; and as for Cap'n Moseby and his gun, she knew he would not shoot her; once he had given her some peppermints.

She pulled her bush down painfully, and thought the berries were not very large, and how fast those in Cap'n Moseby's pasture would fill up. Harriet's and Mary Ann's voices grew fainter. Mirandy let the bush fly back, and pushed softly through a tangle of blackberry vines to the stone-wall; a narrow stretch of rocky land lay between it and the other which bounded Cap'n Moseby's land. Mirandy stood on tiptoe, and peered over; then she looked at Jonathan asleep in his little wagon, his yellow lashes on his pink cheeks, his fat fists doubled up.

Mirandy was loyal, although she was so young, and she had been bidden not to leave Jonathan. She looked at him, then at the stone-wall; it was manifestly impossible for her to lift him over that. She took hold of the little wagon, and pushed it carefully along. She remembered that she had seen some bars a little farther back.

When she reached the bars, she shook Jonathan until he woke up. He stared at her in a surprised way, but never cried; he was a good baby.

"Put your arms round sister's neck," ordered Mirandy; and Jonathan obeyed.

Mirandy tugged him out of his little wagon, and they both rolled over under a berry bush. Still Jonathan did not cry. He only gurgled a little, by way of laugh. He thought Mirandy was playing with him.

The bars were close together, and Mirandy could not stir one. Jonathan gurgled again when his sister rolled him, like a ball, under the lowest bar, and then rolled under herself. But it was harder for her to tug Jonathan across to the other bars which guarded Cap'n Moseby's berry pasture; he could only toddle feebly when led by a strong hand. It was quite a puzzle for six-year-old Mirandy, but she got him across and under the other bars; then she set him down in a sweet-fern thicket, and bade him keep still; and he fell asleep again.

Mirandy picked until she had filled her bucket and rounded it up. Her heart beat faster and faster; her face was flushed and eager; she looked a year older than when she started that morning. She had seen no great black dog, and Cap'n Moseby, with his gun, had not appeared. In the distance she could see the hipped roof and squat chimney of the Moseby house; but nobody molested her.

When her bucket was full, she tugged Jonathan across the field again. This time he rebelled; a blackberry vine had scratched his little legs, and his peace was too rudely disturbed. Mirandy tugged him into his little wagon, and he lay there kicking and screaming. She flew back across the field for her bucket of berries.

She had been forced to leave it while she brought Jonathan over, and the bucket was gone. She had set it close to the bars, and there could be no mistake about it.

Mirandy went back across the field; Jonathan wailed louder than ever. Her four sisters were gathered about his little wagon, and Daniel and Abijah were coming through the bushes. Then they all turned on her.

"Now, Mirandy Thayer, I'd like to know this minute where you've been?" demanded Eliza.

Mirandy jerked her head backward.

"You 'ain't been over in Cap'n Moseby's pasture?"

Mirandy nodded.

"She's been over in Cap'n Moseby's pasture," announced Eliza to the others.

They all stared at Mirandy, and paid no heed to Jonathan's wails.

Suddenly Mirandy flung her little blue apron over her face and began to weep.

"Did you get scared?" asked Harriet.

"Did the dog chase you?" asked Mary Ann, very excitedly.

Mirandy shook her head, and sobbed harder.

"Did you see Cap'n Moseby with his gun?" asked Daniel.

Mirandy shook her head.

"I wouldn't be such a baby for nothing, then," said Daniel.

"I've lost my bucket!" sobbed Mirandy.

"Lost your bucket!" repeated Eliza. She was the oldest sister there.

Mirandy nodded.

"You're a wicked girl!" Eliza said, severely. "I don't know what mother 'll say. Here's Jonathan all scratched up, too. Did you take him over there?"

"Yes," sobbed Mirandy.

"You're a dreadful wicked girl! Didn't you know 'twas stealing?"

"Harriet said—it wasn't," returned Mirandy, in feeble defence.

"It was. I shouldn't think you'd said such a thing, Harriet."

"Of course it's stealing," said Daniel, soberly.

"Here you've been stealing," scolded Eliza; "and your bucket's gone, and Jonathan is all scratched up with blackberry vines. I don't know what mother 'll say."

She took Jonathan out of his wagon and hushed him, and then they had a consultation as to what was best to be done. Mirandy related, with tearful breaks, the story of her well-filled bucket and its mysterious disappearance.

"Of course Cap'n Moseby was watching out there with his gun and took it," said Daniel.

It was finally agreed that they would all go in a body to Cap'n Moseby's, and try to recover Mirandy's bucket, that she might not have to face her mother without it. When they reached the Moseby house the doors were closed and the windows looked blank. They knocked as loudly as they dared, and there was not a sound in response. They looked at one another.

"S'pose he ain't at home?" whispered Harriet.

"Dan'l, you pound on the door again," said Eliza.

And Daniel pounded. Abijah pounded, too, and Eliza herself rattled away on one panel, with her freckled face screwed up, but nobody came.

"If he's there, he won't come to the door," said Daniel.

Suddenly the silence within the house was broken. Then came a volley of quick barks, and the children all fell back in a panic, and scurried into the road.

"He's in there," said Daniel; "an' he's been keeping the dog still, but he can't any longer."

"Just hear him!" whispered Harriet, with a shudder.

The dog was not only barking and growling, but leaping at the door.

"THE VISIT TO CAP'N MOSEBY'S"

Mary Ann began to cry. "I'm going home," she sobbed. "S'pose that door should break;" and she started down the road.

Eliza grasped the handle of Jonathan's wagon. "I guess we might just as well go," she said. "I don't b'lieve he'll come to the door if we stand there a week. I don't know what mother 'll say when she finds that good bucket's gone. I guess Mirandy 'll catch it. An' when she finds out she's been stealing, too, I don't know what she will say."

The sorry procession started. Jonathan's wagon creaked; but Mirandy stood still, with a stubborn pout on her mouth, and her brows contracted over her blue eyes.

"Come along, Mirandy," called Eliza, with a foreboding voice.

But Mirandy stood still.

"Why don't you come?" Harriet said.

"I ain't coming," said Mirandy.

"What?"

"I ain't coming till I get my bucket."

Then the whole procession stopped, and reasoned and argued, but Mirandy was unmoved.

"What are you going to do? You can't get in," said Eliza.

"I'm going to sit on the door-step till Cap'n Moseby comes out," answered Mirandy.

"You'll sit there all day, likely 's not," said Eliza. "What do you s'pose mother 'll say? I'm a-going to tell her."

"She'll send me right back again if I don't stay," said Mirandy.

And there was some show of reason in what she said. It was indeed quite probable that Mrs. Josiah Thayer would send Mirandy straight back again to confess her sins and get the bucket.

"I don't know but mother would send her back," said Eliza; and Daniel nodded in assent.

"I'll stay with you," said Mary Ann, although she was still trembling with fear of the dog.

"Don't want anybody to stay," protested Mirandy.

Finally she sat on Cap'n Moseby's door-step, and watched them all straggle out of sight. The creak of Jonathan's wagon grew fainter and fainter, until she could hear it no longer. The dog was quiet now. Mirandy sat up straight in front of the panelled door.

She waited and waited; the time went on, and it was high noon. She heard a dinner-horn in the distance. She wondered vaguely if Cap'n Moseby didn't have any dinner because he lived alone. She began to feel hungry herself. There was not a sound in the house. She wanted to cry, but she would not. She sat perfectly still.

Once in a while she said over to herself the questions she had learned from the catechism, and she reflected much upon the two boys in the *Pilgrim's Progress*. She had eaten a few of the Cap'n's berries as she filled her bucket, and she wondered that they did not make her ill, as the fruit did the boys.

Nobody passed the house, the insects rasped in her ears, she thought her forlorn childish thoughts, and it was an hour after noon. She did not see a curtain trimmed with white balls in a window overhead pulled cautiously to one side, and a grizzled head thrust out; but this happened several times.

About two o'clock there was a sudden puff of cool wind on her back; she glanced around, trembling, and there stood Cap'n Moseby in the open door, with his great black dog at his heels. His old face was the color of tanned leather, and full of severe furrows; his shaggy brows frowned over sharp black eyes. He leaned upon a stout oak staff, for he had been lamed by a British musket-ball.

"Who's this?" he asked, in a grim voice.

Mirandy arose and stood about, and courtesied. She could not find her tongue yet.

"Hey?" said Cap'n Moseby.

"**Mirandy Thayer**," she answered then, in a

shaking voice that had yet a touch of defiance in it.

"Mirandy Thayer, hey? Well, what do you want here, Mirandy Thayer?"

Mirandy dropped another courtesy. "My bucket."

"Your bucket! What have I got to do with your bucket?"

"I left it out in—your berry pasture."

"Out in my berry pasture! So you have been stealing my berries, hey? What about your bucket?"

Mirandy's little hands clutched and opened at her sides, her face was quite pale, but she looked straight up at Cap'n Moseby. "You took it," said she.

Cap'n Moseby looked straight back at her, frowning terribly; then, to her great astonishment, his mouth twitched as if he were going to laugh. "You think I took your bucket, and you have been waiting here all this time to get it back, hey?" said he.

"Yes, sir."

"Didn't you feel afraid that I'd set the dog on you, or shoot you out of the window with my gun?"

"No, sir," said Mirandy.

"Well," said Cap'n Moseby. He paused a minute, his mouth twitched again. "You have got to come into the house and settle with me if you want your bucket," he continued, and his voice was still very grim.

Mirandy stepped up on the threshold, and the black dog growled faintly.

"Be still, Lafayette!" said Cap'n Moseby. "I'm going to settle with her. You lay down."

She followed Cap'n Moseby into his kitchen, and he pushed a little stool towards her. "Sit down," said he.

And Mirandy sat down. Directly opposite her, on a corner of the settle, was her berry bucket, and near it stood the gun, propped against the wall. She eyed it. There was a vague fear in her mind that settlement was in some way connected with that gun; but she never flinched. She was resolved to have that bucket.

Cap'n Moseby went to the dresser and got out a large china bowl with green sprigs on it, and a pewter spoon. He filled the bowl with berries from Mirandy's bucket, and then poured on some milk out of a blue pitcher. Mirandy watched him.

He carried the bowl over to her, and set it in her lap. "Eat 'em all up, now, every one," he commanded.

Mirandy looked up at him pitifully. Her

courage almost failed. She thought of the boys and the stolen fruit in the *Pilgrim's Progress*, and she almost felt premonitory cramps.

"Eat 'em," ordered Cap'n Moseby.

And Mirandy ate them, thrusting the pewter spoon, laden with those stolen berries, desperately into her mouth. Never berries tasted like those to her. There was no sweetness in them. But she kept thinking how her mother could give her boneset tea if they made her sick, and she was determined to have the bucket back.

Cap'n Moseby watched her as she ate. He emptied the remaining berries out of the bucket into a large bowl. Then he sat opposite, on the settle. Lafayette lay at his feet.

Mirandy finished the berries, and sat with the empty bowl in her lap.

"Finished 'em?" asked Cap'n Moseby.

"Yes, sir."

"Now, Mirandy Thayer, I'm going to ask you a question." Cap'n Moseby's eyes looked into hers, and she looked back into his. "If you hadn't been a little gal, Mirandy Thayer, what would you have been?"

Mirandy hesitated.

"Hey?" said Cap'n Moseby.

"One of my brothers," said Mirandy, doubtfully.

"EAT 'EM!" ORDERED CAP'N MOSEBY

"No, you wouldn't. I'll tell you what you would have been. You would have been a soldier, and you would have gone right up to the redcoats' guns. Well, you must tend to your knittin'-work and your spinnin'. Now what did you steal my berries for, hey?"

"To earn my shoes," faltered Mirandy; she felt a little bewildered.

"Earn your shoes?"

"Yes, sir; I 'ain't got any to wear to meetin'."

"Have to go barefoot?"

"Yes, sir."

"Well, they went barefoot at Valley Forge; that's nothing. You wait a minute, Mirandy Thayer."

And Mirandy waited until Cap'n Moseby had limped into another room and back again. He had a pair of little rough shoes dangling in his hand.

"Here," said he, "these belonged to my Ezra that died. He had some grit in him; he'd have done some marchin' in 'em if he'd lived. They'll jest about fit you. It's a pity you're a little gal. Well, you must tend to your knittin'-work and your spinnin'. Now you'd better run home, an' don't you ever come stealin' my berries again, or you'll run faster than they did at Lexington."

And so it happened that Mirandy went home,

about three o'clock of that summer afternoon, carrying her new shoes in her berry bucket, and Cap'n Moseby limped along at her side. Mirandy did not know that he went to explain matters to her mother, so that she should not be dealt with too severely, but she was surprised that she received so small a chiding.

"Don't you ever let me hear of your doing such a thing again," said her mother; and that was all she said.

The next Sunday Mirandy went up the aisle clattering bravely in little Ezra Moseby's shoes, and she could not help looking often at them during the sermon.

A PARSNIP STEW

Ruth stood by with a dish and spoon, while her mother stirred the stew carefully to be sure that it was not burning on the bottom of the kettle. Her sister Serena was paring apples and playing with the cat, and her father and her uncles Caleb and Silas sat before the fire smoking, sniffing the stew, and watching solemnly. The uncles had just come in, and proposed staying to dinner.

Mrs. Whitman squinted anxiously at the stew as she stirred it. She feared that there was not enough for dinner, now there were two more to eat.

"I'm dreadful afraid there ain't enough of that stew to go round," she whispered to Ruth in the pantry.

"Oh, I guess it 'll do," said Ruth.

"Well, I dun know about it. Your father an' Caleb an' Silas are dreadful fond of parsnip stew, an' I do hate to have 'em stinted."

"Well, I won't take any," said Ruth. "I don't care much about it."

"Well, I don't want a mouthful," rejoined her mother. "Mebbe we can make it do. Caleb an' Silas don't have a good hot dinner very often, an' I do want them to have enough, anyway."

Caleb and Silas Whitman were old bachelors, living by themselves in the old Whitman homestead about a mile away, and their fare was understood to be forlorn and desultory. To-day they watched with grave complacency while their sister-in-law cooked the stew.

Over on the other side of the kitchen the table was set out with the pewter plates and the blue dishes. The stew was almost done, Mrs. Whitman was just about to dip out the slices of pork into the dish that Ruth held, when there was a roll of wheels out in the yard, and a great shadow passed over the kitchen floor.

"Mother, it's the Wigginses!" said Ruth, in a terrified whisper.

"Good gracious!" sighed her mother; "they've come to dinner."

Everybody stared for a second; then Mrs. Whitman recovered herself. "Father, you go out an' help them put the horse up. Don't sit there any longer."

Then she threw open the door, and thrust her

large handsome face out into the rain. "Why, how do you do, Mis' Wiggins?" said she, and she smiled beamingly.

The wagon looked full of faces. On the front seat were a large man and two little boys; out of the gloom in the rear peered two women and a little girl. They were Mr. Wiggins, his wife and three children, and his mother. They were distant relatives of Mrs. Whitman's; they often came over to spend the day, and always unannounced.

Mr. Whitman came out clumsily and opened the barn doors, and Mr. Wiggins led the horse into the barn. "I hope you 'ain't got wet," Mrs. Whitman said. Nothing could have exceeded her cordiality; but all the time she was thinking of the parsnip stew, and how it surely would not go around now.

Ruth had not followed the others out to greet the guests. She stayed by the kettle and stirred the stew, and scowled. "I think it's downright mean for folks to come in this way, just dinner-time," said she to the uncles, who had not left their chairs. And they gave short grunts which expressed their assent, for neither of them liked company.

They watched soberly as Ruth stirred the stew, but they did not dream that there was not enough to go around.

When her mother and the guests entered, Ruth turned around and bobbed her head stiffly, and said, "Pretty well, thank you," and then stirred again. Serena helped the Wigginses take off their things. She untied old Mrs. Wiggins's pumpkin hood, and got her cap out of her cap basket and put it on for her. She also took off little Mary Wiggins's coat, and set her in a little child's arm-chair and gave her a kiss. Little Mary Wiggins, with her sober, chubby face and her rows of shiny brown curls, in her best red frock and her scalloped pantalets, was noticed admiringly by everybody but Ruth.

As soon as she could Ruth cornered her mother in the pantry. "Mother, what *are* you going to do?" said she.

"I'm goin' to do jest the best I can," she whispered, severely. "I'm goin' to tell father an' Caleb an' Silas they mustn't take none of that stew; they can have some bread an' apple-sauce. I guess they'll git along."

"Well, I don't care," said Ruth, in a loud voice. "I think it's mean and a downright imposition on folks, coming in this way, just dinner-time."

"Ruth Whitman, if you care anything about me, you'll keep still. Now you get the salt-cup an' go out there, an' put some more salt in that stew. It tasted dreadful flat, I thought. I jest tasted of it when they drove in. I've got to get out the other knives."

Ruth caught up a cup with a jerk. "Well, how much shall I put in?" she inquired, sulkily.

"Oh, quite a lot. You can tell. It was dreadful flat. Taste of it."

But Ruth did not taste of it. She scattered the contents of the cup liberally into the stew, gave it a stir, returned to the pantry, and set the cup down hard. "Well," said she, "I've put it in, and now I'm goin'."

"Ruth Whitman, you ain't goin' off to school without any dinner."

"I don't see as there is anything for dinner but bread and apple-sauce, and I'm sure I don't want any."

"I should think you'd be ashamed of yourself, actin' so."

"I think there are other folks that ought to be ashamed of themselves. Before I'd go into folk's houses that way—"

"Ruth Whitman, they'll hear you!"

"I don't care if they do. I've got to go, anyway. It's late. I couldn't stop for dinner now if I wanted to."

She went through the kitchen, where Serena now tended the stew, only stopping to take her shawl off the peg.

"Why, you going?" Serena called after her.

"I've got to; it's late," replied Ruth, shortly. She faced about for a second and gave a stiff nod, which seemed directed at the stew-kettle rather than at the Wigginses. "Good-bye," said she. Then she went out.

It was raining with a hard, steady drizzle. Ruth had no rubbers nor water-proof—they were not yet invented. She sped along through the rain and mist. She had to walk half a mile to the little house where she taught the district school, and before she got there she felt calmer.

"I suppose I was silly to act so mad," she said to herself. "I know it plagued mother."

It was early in the spring; the trees were turning green in the rain. Over in the field she could see one peach-tree in blossom, showing pink through the mist. "I suppose Mr. Wiggins couldn't work out to-day, and that's how they happened to come. They could have the horse. But they ought to have come earlier," reflected Ruth. "There are a good many of 'em for Mrs. Wiggins to get ready," mused Ruth. "There's old Mrs. Wiggins and Johnny and Sammy and Mary and Mr. Wiggins."

By the time Ruth was seated at her table in the school-room, and the scholars were wriggling and twisting before her on their wooden benches, she saw the matter quite plainly from the Wigginses side. She made up her mind that she would behave just as well as she knew how to the Wigginses when she got home. She planned how she would swing little Mary out in the barn and play with the boys, and how she would help her mother get tea.

When school was done and Ruth started for home the rain had stopped and the sun was shining. The rain-pools in the road glittered, and she noticed a cherry-tree in blossom. When she reached home Serena met her at the door.

"Oh, Ruth Whitman!" she cried, we have had such a time!"

Ruth stared. "What do you mean?" said she. "Where are the Wigginses?"

"They've gone. Mrs. Wiggins and old Mrs. Wiggins were dreadful mad. Oh, Ruth, you didn't do it on purpose, did you?"

"Do what on purpose?" said Ruth, pushing into the house, and looking around the empty kitchen in a bewildered way. "I don't know what you mean."

"Don't you know what you put into that parsnip stew?"

"No; I don't know of anything I put in but some salt, just before I went to school; mother told me to. Why?"

"Oh, Ruth, you put in—saleratus!"

"I don't believe it."

Ruth flew into the pantry, and came out with a cracked blue cup. "Here," said she—"here's the salt-cup, and this is the one I got it out of, I know."

"Taste of it," said Serena, solemnly.

Ruth tasted. "It *is* saleratus," said she, looking at her sister in horror. "Did it spoil the stew?"

"It was—dreadful."

"I don't see how it happened," Ruth said, slowly, puckering her forehead, "unless mother dipped out some saleratus in the salt-cup to bring out in the kitchen when she mixed the sour-milk cakes for breakfast. I don't know anything about it, true 's I live and breathe. I hope they didn't think I did such a mean thing as that on purpose."

"Well, I don't know as they really thought you did, but you know you did kind of jerk round, Ruth, and the Wigginses saw it."

"What did they say?"

"Well," said Serena, "we all sat down to the table, and mother had put on the bread and apple-sauce for the rest of us, and she helped the Wigginses to the stew. There wasn't more'n enough to go around, but she kept the cover over the dish so they shouldn't suspect, and all the rest of us said we wouldn't take any.

"Well, Mrs. Wiggins she tasted, and old Mrs. Wiggins she tasted. Then they looked at mother. Mother she didn't know what it meant, and she kept getting redder and redder. Finally she spoke up. 'Is there anything the matter with the stew?' says she.

"Then Mrs. Wiggins she pushed over her plate for mother to taste of the stew, and the first thing we knew they were all talking at once. Old Mrs. Wiggins said she'd noticed how we acted kind of stiff, and as if we wasn't glad to see them, the minute she come, and Mrs. Wiggins said she had, too, and she'd seen you put the saleratus into the stew, and she thought from the way you switched around you were up to something. Mother she tried to excuse it off, but they wouldn't hear a word. They said it didn't look very likely that it was an accident, and they noticed none of us took any of it, and mother wouldn't tell them the reason for that. So they just got up and put on their things, and Mr. Wiggins backed out the horse, and they went home. Mother asked them to come again, and she'd try and have a better dinner, but they said they'd never set foot in the house again if they knew it."

"Didn't anybody eat the stew?"

"Nobody but Sammy Wiggins; he ate his whole plateful, saleratus and all, before anybody spoke."

"Oh dear!" said Ruth; "I suppose mother feels dreadfully. Where is she?"

"She's gone over to Lucy Ann's to help her take care of the baby; he was real sick last night. I don't believe she'll come home till after supper. She felt dreadful."

"The Wigginses are dreadful touchy folks, anyhow."

"Course they are. It don't seem as if anybody with any sense would get mad at such a thing. But they're always suspecting folks of meaning something."

Ruth looked sternly reflective. She took off her thick dingy shawl, and got from its peg a bright red and green plaid one that she wore in pleasant weather.

"Where are you going?" asked Serena.

"I'm going over to the Wigginses'."

"What for?"

"I'm going to ask them to come over here tomorrow and spend the day."

"Why, Ruth Whitman, ain't you afraid to?"

"No, I ain't afraid. I'm going to carry over a jar of the honey—mother 'll be willing—and I'm going to tell Mrs. Wiggins just how it was."

"She won't hear a word you say."

"I'll make her hear."

"They won't come a step."

"You see."

The Whitmans kept bees, and their honey was the celebrated luxury of the neighborhood. Ruth got a jar of clear white honey out of the closet, put it under her shawl, and was off. First, though, she instructed Serena to go out in the garden and dig a good supply of parsnips and clean them for the next day's dinner.

It was a mile to the Wigginses', and it took Ruth over an hour to accomplish her errand and return. When she got home she found Serena getting supper, and her father was washing his hands out in the shed; her mother had not returned. On the kitchen sink lay a tin pan with four or five muddy parsnips. Serena looked up eagerly when her sister entered. "They coming?" said she.

"Yes, they are," replied Ruth, with a triumphant smile.

But Serena walked over to the sink and extended her arm with a tragical gesture towards the parsnips. "Well, you've gone and done it now, Ruth Whitman," said she. "There's every single parsnip that's fit to eat that I could find in the garden."

"H'm! I guess I can find some."

"No, you can't; they've rotted. I heard mother say to-day she was afraid they had. More'n half those father brought in this morning weren't good for anything. When mother finds out that all the Wigginses are coming, and there's just five parsnips for dinner, I don't know what she will do; I don't know but it will kill her. And she's asked Uncle Caleb and Uncle Silas over, too."

Ruth gave a desperate glance at the parsnips. "I said we were going to have parsnip stew," said she. "Mrs. Wiggins had been crying; she looked dreadful tired out; and Sammy had just bumped his head, and there was a great lump over one eye. She took the honey, and said she'd be real happy to come if they could have the horse, and old Mrs. Wiggins acted dreadful tickled."

"The Wigginses have got parsnips," said Serena. "I heard Mrs. Wiggins say they'd got a splendid lot, she expected, but they hadn't dug any yet."

Ruth looked at her sister. "Serena!"

"What?"

"I'm going to send over and *buy some of the Wigginses' parsnips*."

"Ruth!" But it seemed to Serena as if there was a flash of red and green light through the room, and Ruth had gone. Serena gave a little gasp, and stood looking.

"What's the matter?" asked her father, coming in — an old man in checkered shirt sleeves, yet with a certain rustic stateliness about him.

"Oh, nothing," said Serena; and she fell to slicing the bread for supper.

While her father had gone to the well to draw a pail of water Ruth came in, breathless, but rosy with daring and triumph. Ben White, Mrs. White's grown-up son, was going to drive over to the Wigginses and buy some parsnips; his mother was to have some, and Ruth a noble portion for the next day's stew.

Serena dropped into a chair and giggled feebly; the humor of it was so forcible that it seemed to fairly rebound in her face. "Ask the Wigginses to dinner to have a parsnip stew, and then—buy their own parsnips for it!" she gasped.

Ruth did not laugh at all; she saw nothing but the seriousness of the situation. "Mind you don't tell mother till after it's all over," said she. "I don't want her to know where those parsnips came from till after the Wigginses have gone, she'll be so upset. I'm just going to tell her how I carried the honey over there, and how they're coming. I do hope Ben will bring the parsnips before mother gets home."

"Suppose Ben should bring 'em in when mother was here," chuckled Serena.

"I told him to shy into the shed with 'em," replied Ruth, severely. "Hush! father's coming, and we'd better not say anything to him till afterwards."

Mrs. Whitman did not return until quite late; her married daughter Lucy Ann and her teething baby did not generally release her in very good season. When she came into the kitchen she found a great pan of parsnips all washed and scraped, and heard the news how the Wigginses were over their ill-tempers and were coming the next day. Mrs. Whitman dropped into a chair, her large mild face beamed, and tears stood in her eyes. "Well, I'm dreadful glad if we can patch it up," said she; "I never had any fuss with any of my folks before in the world, and I hate to begin now. I've always thought a good deal of the Wigginses." And her mouth quivered.

The next morning a parsnip stew of noble proportions was prepared. At eleven o'clock the great kettle, full to the rim, hung over the fire, and the room was cloudy with savory steam. The Wigginses were expected every minute. Uncles Silas and Caleb Whitman could be seen from the kitchen window out in the field with their brother bending over the plough furrows, and they kept righting themselves and looking at their old silver watches. At half-past eleven Mrs. Whitman and Serena began to think it was strange that the Wigginses did not come. At quarter of twelve there was a little stir out in the yard, and they ran to the windows. There was Mr. Wiggins with a wheelbarrow and an empty grain sack and a half-bushel basket of russet apples in it.

Mrs. Whitman and Serena stood wonderingly in the door. "Where's the folks?" asked Mrs. Whitman.

Then Mr. Wiggins, standing by the wheelbarrow, explained how Hiram Green had had to use the horse for ploughing up in the six-acre lot, how he had promised to hire it to him, and his wife hadn't known it, and how he had had to go to the store for grain with the wheelbarrow, and his wife had got him to stop and tell Mis' Whitman she was dreadfully sorry it happened so, but she didn't see how they could walk, and they would come over the first day they could have the horse; and she didn't know but what Mis' Whitman's apples had give out, so she sent her over a few of their russets; they had 'most two barrels left, and they were spoiling fast, and they wanted to get rid of them.

When Ruth came home from school she found an immense kettle of parsnip stew, her father and her uncles Silas and Caleb again forming a pleasant expectant semicircle before the fire, but no Wigginses. To-day the stew was seasoned daintily, and salt had taken the place of saleratus. There was no stint as to quantity, but there were not enough partakers. Mrs. Whitman filled a great bowl for Lucy Ann; she sent a dish over to the Whites; father and Caleb and Silas ate manfully, and passed their plates again and again; Serena and Ruth and their mother ate all they could, and the cat had her fill; but the Whitmans, with all their allies, could not eat their own share and that of the Wigginses. But the stew was delicious, and as the family ate, their simple homely little feud was healed, and the parsnip stew smoked in their midst like a pipe of peace.

THE DICKEY BOY

"I should think it was about time for him to be comin'," said Mrs. Rose.

"So should I," assented Miss Elvira Grayson. She peered around the corner of the front door. Her face was thin and anxious, and her voice was so like it that it was unmistakably her own note. One would as soon expect a crow to chick-a-dee as Miss Elvira to talk in any other way. She was tall, and there was a sort of dainty angularity about her narrow shoulders. She wore an old black silk, which was a great deal of dress for afternoon. She had considerable money in the bank, and could afford to dress well. She wore also some white lace around her long neck, and it was fastened with a handsome gold-and-jet brooch. She was knitting some blue worsted, and she sat back in the front entry, out of the draft. She considered herself rather delicate.

Mrs. Rose sat boldly out in the yard in the full

range of the breeze, sewing upon a blue-and-white gingham waist for her son Willy. She was a large, pretty-faced woman in a stiffly starched purple muslin, which spread widely around her.

"He's been gone 'most an hour," she went on; "I hope there's nothin' happened."

"I wonder if there's snakes in that meadow?" ruminated Miss Elvira.

"I don't know; I'm gettin' ruther uneasy."

"I know one thing—I shouldn't let him go off so, without somebody older with him, if he was my boy."

"Well, I don't know what I can do," returned Mrs. Rose, uneasily. "There ain't anybody to go with him. I can't go diggin' sassafras-root, and you can't, and his uncle Hiram's too busy, and grandfather is too stiff. And he is so crazy to go after sassafras-root, it does seem a pity to tell him he sha'n't. I never saw a child so possessed after the root and sassafras-tea, as he is, in my life. I s'pose it's good for him. I hate to deny him when he takes so much comfort goin'. There he is now!"

Little Willy Rose crossed the road, and toiled up the stone steps. The front yard was terraced, and two flights of stone steps led up to the front door. He was quite breathless when he stood on the top step; his round, sweet face was pink, his fair hair plastered in flat locks to his wet forehead. His little trousers and his shoes were muddy, and he carried a great scraggy mass of sassafras-roots. "I see you a-settin' out here," he panted, softly.

"You ought not to have stayed so long. We began to be worried about you," said his mother, in a fond voice. "Now go and take your muddy shoes right off, and put on your slippers; then you can sit down at the back door and clean your sassafras, if you want to."

"I got lots," said Willy, smiling sweetly, and wiping his forehead. "Look-a-there, Miss Elviry."

"So you did," returned Miss Elvira. "I suppose, now, you think you'll have some sassafras-tea."

"Yes, ma'am."

"I guess I'll steep him a little for supper, he's so crazy for it," said Mrs. Rose, when Willy had disappeared smilingly around the corner.

"Yes, I would. It's real wholesome for him. Who's that comin'?"

Mrs. Rose stared down at the road. A white horse with an open buggy was just turning into the drive-way, around the south side of the terraces. "Why, it's brother Hiram," said she, "and he's got a boy with him. I wonder who 'tis."

The buggy drew up with a grating noise in the drive-way. Presently a man appeared around the corner. After him tagged a small white-headed boy, and after the boy, Willy Rose, with a sassafras-root and an old shoe-knife in his hands.

The man, who was Mr. Hiram Fairbanks, Mrs. Rose's brother, had a somewhat doubtful expression. When he stopped, the white-headed boy stopped, keeping a little behind him in his shadow.

"What boy is that, Hiram?" asked Mrs. Rose. Miss Elvira peered around the door. Mr. Fairbanks was tall and stiff-looking. He had a sun-burned, sober face. "His name is Dickey," he replied.

"One of those Dickeys?" Mrs. Rose said "Dickeys," as if it were a synonym for "outcasts" or "rascals."

Mr. Fairbanks nodded. He glanced at the boy in his wake, then at Willy. "Willy, s'pose you take this little boy 'round and show him your rabbits," he said, in an embarrassed voice.

"Willy Rose!" cried his mother, "you haven't changed those muddy shoes! Go right in this minute, 'round by the kitchen door, and take this boy 'round with you; he can sit down on the door-step and help you clean your sassafras-root."

Willy disappeared lingeringly around the house, and the other boy, on being further bidden by Mr. Fairbanks, followed him. "Willy," his mother cried after him, "mind you sit down on the door-step and tie your shoes! I ain't goin' to have that Dickey boy left alone; his folks are nothin' but a pack of thieves," she remarked in a lower tone. "What are you doing with him, Hiram?"

Hiram hesitated. "Well, 'Mandy, you was sayin' the other day that you wished you had a boy to run errands, and split up kindlin's, and be kind of company for Willy."

"You ain't brought that Dickey boy?"

"Now, look here, 'Mandy—"

"I ain't going to have him in the house."

"Jest look here a minute, 'Mandy, till I tell you how it happened, and then you can do jest as you're a mind to about it. I was up by the Ruggles's this afternoon, and Mis' Ruggles, she come out to the gate, and hailed me. She wanted to know if I didn't want a boy. Seems the Dickey woman died last week; you know the father died two year ago. Well, there was six children, and the oldest boy 's skipped, nobody knows where, and the oldest girl has just got married, and this boy is the oldest of the four that's left. They took the three little ones to the poorhouse, and Mis' Ruggles she took this boy in, and she wanted to keep him, but her own boy is big enough to do all the chores, and she didn't feel as if she could afford to. She says he's a real nice little fellow, and his mother wa'n't a bad woman; she was jest kind of sickly and shiftless. I guess old Dickey wa'n't much, but he's dead. Mis' Ruggles says this little chap hates awful to go to the poorhouse, and it ain't no kind of risk to take him, and she'd ought to know. She's lived right there next door to the Dickeys ever since she was married. I knew you wanted a boy to do chores 'round, long as Willy wasn't strong enough, so I thought I'd fetch him along. But you can do jest as you're a mind to."

"Now, Hiram Fairbanks, you know the name those Dickeys have always had. S'pose I took that boy, and he stole?"

"Mis' Ruggles says she'd trust him with anything."

"She ain't got so much as I have to lose. There I've got two dozen solid silver teaspoons, and four table-spoons, and my mother's silver creamer, and Willy's silver napkin-ring. Elviry's got her gold watch, too."

"I've got other things I wouldn't lose for anything," chimed in Miss Elvira.

"Well, of course, I don't want you to lose anything," said Mr. Fairbanks, helplessly, "but Mis' Ruggles, she said he was perfectly safe."

"I s'pose I could lock up the silver spoons and use the old pewter ones, and Elviry could keep her watch out of sight for a while," ruminated Mrs. Rose.

"Yes, I could," assented Miss Elvira, "and my breastpin."

"I s'pose he could draw the water, and split up the kindlin'-wood, and weed the flower-garden," said Mrs. Rose. "I set Willy to weedin' this morning, and it gave him the headache. I tell you one thing, Hiram Fairbanks, if I do take this boy, you've got to stand ready to take him back again the first minute I see anything out of the way with him."

"Yes, I will, 'Mandy; I promise you I will," said Mr. Fairbanks, eagerly. He hurried out to the buggy, and fumbled under the seat; then he returned with a bundle and a small wooden box.

"Here's his clothes. I guess he ain't got much," said he.

Mrs. Rose took the newspaper bundle; then she eyed the box suspiciously. It was a wooden salt-box, and the sliding cover was nailed on.

"What's in this?" said she.

"Oh, I don't know," replied Mr. Fairbanks; "some truck or other—I guess it ain't worth much."

He put the box down on the bank, and trudged heavily and quickly out to the buggy. He was anxious to be off; he shook the reins, shouted "ge lang" to the white horse, and wheeled swiftly around the corner.

"I'd like to know what's in that box," said Mrs. Rose to Miss Elvira.

"I hope he ain't got an old pistol or anything of that kind in it," returned Miss Elvira. "Oh, 'Mandy, I wouldn't shake it, if I were you!" For Mrs. Rose was shaking the wooden box, and listening with her ear at it.

"Something rattles in it," said she, desisting; "I hope it ain't a pistol." Then she entered with the newspaper bundle and the box, and went through the house, with Miss Elvira following. She set the bundle and box on the kitchen table, and looked out of the door. There on the top step sat the Dickey boy cleaning the sassafras-roots with great industry, while Willy Rose sat on the lower one chewing some.

"I do believe he's goin' to take right hold, Elviry," whispered Mrs. Rose.

"Well, maybe he is," returned Miss Elvira.

Mrs. Rose stowed away the boy's belongings in the little bedroom off the kitchen where she meant him to sleep; then she kindled the fire and got supper. She made sassafras-tea, and the new boy, sitting beside Willy, had a cup poured for him. But he did not drink much nor eat much, although there were hot biscuits and berries and custards. He hung his forlorn head with its shock of white hair, and only gave fleeting glances at anything with his wild, blue eyes. He was a thin boy, smaller than Willy, but he looked wiry and full of motion, like a wild rabbit.

After supper Mrs. Rose sent him for a pail of water; then he split up a little pile of kindling-wood. After that he sat down on the kitchen door-step in the soft twilight, and was silent.

Willy went into the sitting-room, where his mother and Miss Elvira were. "He's settin' out there on the door-step, not speakin' a word," said he, in a confidential whisper.

"Well, you had better sit down here with us and read your Sunday-school book," said his mother. She and Miss Elvira had agreed that it was wiser that Willy should not be too much with the Dickey boy until they knew him better.

When it was nine o'clock Mrs. Rose showed the Dickey boy his bedroom. She looked at him sharply; his small pale face showed red stains in the lamplight. She thought to herself that he had been crying, and she spoke to him as kindly as she could—she had not a caressing manner with anybody but Willy. "I guess there's clothes enough on the bed," said she. She looked curiously at the bundle and the wooden box. Then she unfastened the bundle. "I guess I'll see what you've got for clothes," said she, and her tone was as motherly as she could make it towards this outcast Dickey boy. She laid out his pitiful little wardrobe, and examined the small ragged shirt or two and the fragmentary stockings. "I guess I shall have to buy you some things if you are a good boy," said she. "What have you got in that box?"—the boy hung his head—"I hope you ain't got a pistol?"

"No, marm."

"You ain't got any powder, nor anything of that kind?"

"No, marm." The boy was blushing confusedly.

"I hope you're tellin' me the truth," Mrs. Rose said, and her tone was full of severe admonition.

"Yes, marm." The tears rolled down the boy's cheeks, and Mrs. Rose said no more. She told him she would call him in the morning, and to be careful about his lamp. Then she left him. The Dickey boy lay awake, and cried an hour; then he went to sleep, and slept as soundly as Willy Rose in his snug little bedroom leading out of his mother's room. Miss Elvira and Mrs. Rose locked their doors that night, through distrust of that little boy down-stairs who came of a thieving family. Miss Elvira put her gold watch and her breastpin and her pocket-book, with seventeen dollars in it, under the feather-bed; and Mrs. Rose carried the silver teaspoons up-stairs, and hid them under hers. The Dickey boy was not supposed to know they were in the house—the pewter ones had been used for supper—but that did not signify; she thought it best to be on the safe side. She kept the silver spoons under the feather-bed for many a day, and they all ate with the pewter ones; but finally suspicion was allayed if not destroyed. The Dickey boy had shown himself trustworthy in several instances. Once he was sent on a test errand to the store, and came home promptly with the right change. The silver spoons glittered in the spoon-holder on the table, and Miss Elvira wore her gold watch and her gold breastpin.

"I begin to take a good deal more stock in that boy," Mrs. Rose told her brother Hiram.

"He ain't very lively, but he works real smart; he ain't saucy, and I ain't known of his layin' hands on a thing."

But the Dickey boy, although he had won some confidence and good opinions, was, as Mrs. Rose said, not very lively. His face, as he did his little tasks, was as sober and serious as an old man's. Everybody was kind to him, but this poor little alien felt like a chimney-sweep in a queen's palace. Mrs. Rose, to a Dickey boy, was almost as impressive as a queen. He watched with admiration and awe this handsome, energetic woman moving about the house in her wide skirts. He was overcome with the magnificence of Miss Elvira's afternoon silk, and gold watch; and dainty little Willy Rose seemed to him like a small prince. Either the Dickey boy, born in a republican country, had the original instincts of the peasantry in him, and himself defined his place so clearly that it made him unhappy, or his patrons did it for him. Mrs. Rose and Miss Elvira tried to treat him as well as they treated Willy. They dressed him in Willy's old clothes; they gave him just as much to eat; when autumn came he was sent to school as warmly clad and as well provided with luncheon; but they could never forget that he was a Dickey boy. He seemed, in truth, to them like an animal of another species, in spite of all they could do, and they regarded his virtues in the light of uncertain tricks. Mrs. Rose never thought at any time of leaving him in the house alone without hiding the spoons, and Miss Elvira never left her gold watch unguarded.

Nobody knew whether the Dickey boy was aware of these lurking suspicions or not; he was so subdued that it was impossible to tell how much he observed. Nobody knew how homesick he was, but he went about every day full of fierce hunger for his miserable old home. Miserable as it had been, there had been in it a certain element of shiftless ease and happiness. The Dickey boy's sickly mother had never chided him; she had not cared if he tracked mud into the house. How anxiously he scraped his feet before entering the Rose kitchen. The Dickey boy's dissipated father had been gentle and maudlin, but never violent. All the Dickey children had done as they chose, and they had agreed well. They were not a quarrelsome family. Their principal faults were idleness and a general laxity of morals which was quite removed from active wickedness. "All the Dickeys needed was to be bolstered up," one woman in the village said; and the Dickey boy was being bolstered up in the Rose family.

They called him Dickey, using his last name for his first, which was Willy. Mrs. Rose straightened herself unconsciously when she found that out. "We can't have two Willies in the family, anyhow," said she; "we'll have to call you Dickey."

Once the Dickey boy's married sister came to see him, and Mrs. Rose treated her with such stiff politeness that the girl, who was fair and pretty and gaudily dressed, told her husband when she got home that she would never go into *that* woman's house again. Occasionally Mrs. Rose, who felt a duty in the matter, took Dickey to visit his little brothers and sisters at the almshouse. She even bought some peppermint-candy for him to take them. He really had many a little extra kindness shown him; sometimes Miss Elvira gave him a penny, and once Mr. Hiram Fairbanks gave him a sweet-apple tree—that was really quite a magnificent gift. Mrs. Rose could hardly believe it when Willy told her. "Well, I must say I never thought Hiram would do such a thing as that, close as he is," said she. "I was terribly taken aback when he gave that tree to Willy, but this beats all. Why, odd years it might bring in twenty dollars!"

"Uncle Hiram gave it to him," Willy repeated. "I was a-showin' Dickey my apple-tree, and

Uncle Hiram he picked out another one, and he give it to him."

"Well, I wouldn't have believed it," said Mrs. Rose.

Nobody else would have believed that Hiram Fairbanks, careful old bachelor that he was, would have been so touched by the Dickey boy's innocent, wistful face staring up at the boughs of Willy's apple-tree. It was fall, and the apples had all been harvested. Dickey would get no practical benefit from his tree until next season, but there was no calculating the comfort he took with it from the minute it came into his possession. Every minute he could get, at first, he hurried off to the orchard and sat down under its boughs. He felt as if he were literally under his own roof-tree. In the winter, when it was heavy with snow, he did not forsake it. There would be a circle of little tracks around the trunk.

Mrs. Rose told her brother that the boy was perfectly crazy about that apple-tree, and Hiram grinned shamefacedly.

All winter Dickey went with Willy to the district school, and split wood and brought water between times. Sometimes of an evening he sat soberly down with Willy and played checkers, but Willy always won. "He don't try to beat," Willy said. Sometimes they had popcorn, and Dickey always shook the popper. Dickey said he wasn't tired, if they asked him. All winter the silver spoons appeared on the table, and Dickey was treated with a fair show of confidence. It was not until spring that the sleeping suspicion of him awoke. Then one day Mrs. Rose counted her silver spoons, and found only twenty-three teaspoons. She stood at her kitchen table, and counted them over and over. Then she opened the kitchen door. "Elviry!" she called out, "Elviry, come here a minute! Look here," she said, in a hushed voice, when Miss Elvira's inquiring face had appeared at the door. Miss Elvira approached the table tremblingly.

"Count those spoons," said Mrs. Rose.

Miss Elvira's long slim fingers handled the jingling spoons. "There ain't but twenty-three," she said finally, in a scared voice.

"I expected it," said Mrs. Rose. "Do you s'pose he took it?"

"Who else took it, I'd like to know?"

It was a beautiful May morning; the apple-trees were all in blossom. The Dickey boy had stolen over to look at his. It was a round hill of pink-and-white bloom. It was the apple year. Willy came to the stone wall and called him.

"Dickey," he cried, "Mother wants you;" and Dickey obeyed. Willy had run on ahead. He found Mrs. Rose, Miss Elvira, Willy, and the twenty-three teaspoons awaiting him in the kitchen. He shook his head to every question they asked him about the missing spoon. He turned quite pale; once in a while he whimpered; the tears streamed down his cheeks, but he only shook his head in that mute denial.

"It won't make it any easier for you, holding out this way," said Mrs. Rose, harshly. "Stop cryin' and go out and split up some kindlin'-wood."

Dickey went out, his little convulsed form bent almost double. Willy, staring at him with his great, wondering blue eyes, stood aside to let him pass. Then he also was sent on an errand, while his mother and Miss Elvira had a long consultation in the kitchen.

It was a half-hour before Mrs. Rose went out to the shed where she had sent the Dickey boy to split kindlings. There lay a nice little pile of kindlings, but the boy had disappeared.

"Dickey, Dickey!" she called. But he did not come.

"I guess he's gone, spoon and all," she told Miss Elvira, when she went in; but she did not really think he had. When one came to think of it, he was really too small and timid a boy to run away with one silver spoon. It did not seem reasonable. What they did think, as time went on and he did not appear, was that he was hiding to escape a whipping. They searched everywhere. Miss Elvira stood in the shed by the wood-pile, calling in her thin voice, "Come out, Dickey; we won't whip you if you *did* take it," but there was not a stir.

Towards night they grew uneasy. Mr. Fairbanks came, and they talked matters over.

"Maybe he didn't take the spoon," said Mr. Fairbanks, uncomfortably. "Anyhow, he's too young a chap to be set adrift this way. I wish you'd let me talk to him, 'Mandy."

"*You!*" said Mrs. Rose. Then she started up. "I know one thing," said she; "I'm goin' to see what's in that wooden box. I don't believe but what that spoon's in there. There's no knowin' how long it's been gone."

It was quite a while before Mrs. Rose returned with the wooden box. She had to search for it, and found it under the bed. The Dickey boy also had hidden his treasures. She got the hammer and Hiram pried off the lid, which was quite securely nailed. "I'd ought to have had it opened before," said she. "He hadn't no business to have a nailed-up box 'round. Don't jog-

"THERE, AMONG THE BLOSSOMING BRANCHES, CLUNG THE DICKEY BOY."

gle it so, Hiram. There's no knowin' what's in it. There may be a pistol."

Miss Elvira stood farther off. Mr. Fairbanks took the lid entirely off. They all peered into the box. There lay an old clay pipe and a roll of faded calico. Mr. Fairbanks took up the roll and shook it out. "It's an apron," said he. "It's his father's pipe, and his mother's apron—I—swan!"

Miss Elvira began to cry. "I hadn't any idea of anything of that kind," said Mrs. Rose, huskily. "Willy Rose, what *have* you got there?"

For Willy, looking quite pale and guilty, was coming in, holding a muddy silver teaspoon. "Where did you get that spoon? Answer me this minute" cried his mother.

"I—took it out to—dig in my garden with the—other day. I—forgot—"

"Oh, you naughty boy!" cried his mother. Then she, too, began to weep. Mr. Fairbanks started up. "Something's got to be done," said he. "The wind's changed, and the May storm is comin' on. That boy has got to be found before night."

But all Mr. Fairbanks's efforts, and the neighbors' who came to his assistance, could not find the Dickey boy before night or before the next morning. The long, cold May storm began, the flowering apple-trees bent under it, and the wind drove the rain against the windows. Mrs. Rose and Miss Elvira kept the kitchen fire all night, and hot water and blankets ready. But the day had fairly dawned before they found the Dickey boy, and then only by the merest chance. Mr. Fairbanks, hurrying across his orchard for a short cut, and passing Dickey's tree, happened to glance up at it, with a sharp pang of memory. He stopped short. There, among the blossoming branches, clung the Dickey boy, like a little drenched, storm-beaten bird. He had flown to his one solitary possession for a refuge. He was almost exhausted; his little hands grasped a branch like steel claws. Mr. Fairbanks took him down and carried him home. "He was up in his tree," he told his sister, brokenly, when he entered the kitchen. "He's 'most gone."

But the Dickey boy revived after he had lain a while before a fire and been rolled in hot blankets and swallowed some hot drink. He looked with a wondering smile at Mrs. Rose when she bent over him and kissed him just as she kissed Willy. Miss Elvira loosened her gold watch, with its splendid, long gold chain, and put it in his hand. "There, hold it a while," said she, "and listen to it tick." Mr. Fairbanks fumbled in his pocket-book and drew out a great silver dollar. "There," said he, "you can have that to spend when you get well."

Willy pulled his mother's skirt. "Mother," he whispered.

"What say?"

"Can't I pop some corn for him?"

"By-and-by." Mrs. Rose smoothed the Dickey boy's hair; then she bent down and kissed him again. She had fairly made room for him in her stanch, narrow New England heart.

A SWEET-GRASS BASKET

Nancy and Flora were going through the garden, stepping between the squash and tomato vines. Nancy's mother stood in the kitchen door looking after them.

"Mind you don't hit your clothes on the tomatoes!" she called out.

"No, we won't," they answered back. After they had passed the last bean pole they walked single file along the foot-path down the hill. The tall timothy-grass rustled up almost to their waists. Flora went first, with a light little tilt of her starched skirts. Nancy trudged briskly and sturdily after. Nancy's old buff calico dress, which had been let down for her every spring since she was seven years old, and marked its age, like a tree, by rings of a brighter color where the old tucks had been, did not look very well beside Flora's pretty new blue cambric. Neither did Nancy's old Shaker bonnet show to advantage beside Flora's hat, with its beautiful bows and streamers; but Nancy was not troubled about that. She cared very little what she wore, so long as she went somewhere. Flora always had nicer things, but she never minded. Flora was her cousin; she had come to live with her when her mother died, ten years before, and her father had considerable money. He lived in the city.

The two girls were nearly the same age, but Nancy was much the larger; she looked clumsy and overgrown following slender little Flora. It was like a dandelion in the wake of a violet. After they had reached the foot of the hill, they crossed some low meadow-land. It was quite wet, little dark pools glimmered between the clumps of rank grasses. Some fine pink orchid flowers were very thick, but they did not stop to pick any. They were going to see the Indians. Their eyes were fixed upon some white tents ahead. They had been there once before with Nancy's father, but the same sensations of curiosity and exhilarating fear were upon them now.

"Nancy," whispered Flora, fearfully.

"What say?"

"*Is* that a—tomahawk in that tent door?"

"No; it's a hoe," returned Nancy, peering with anxious eyes.

Several Indian women and children were moving about; one Indian man was scraping some birch bark at a tent door. They did not pay any attention to the visitors.

Flora nudged Nancy. "Go along," said she.

"No, you," returned Nancy, pushing Flora.

"I don't dare to."

They stood hesitating. Finally Nancy gave her head a jerk. "I don't care; I'm going, if you ain't," said she, and forward she went. Flora followed.

The tents were arranged like houses on a street, with the open doors fronting each other. In each tent was a counter loaded with baskets and little birch-bark canoes, and an Indian woman sat behind it to sell them.

The girls went from one tent to another and stared about them. Besides the baskets and canoes, there were sea-gulls' wings and little fur slippers and pouches. They saw everything. The Indian women offered to sell, but they shook their heads shyly and soberly.

Finally they went into the tent where the Princess kept store. She was a large stout woman and a real Indian Princess. Under the counter a little Indian baby, fast asleep, was swinging in a tiny hammock. Nancy and Flora nudged each other and eyed it with awe. But it was on the Princess's counter that they saw *the* sweet-grass basket. They both looked at it, then at each other. It was made of sweet-grass, it was oblong, and had a cover and long handles.

Finally Flora pointed one slim little finger at it. "How much does that cost?" she asked the Princess.

"Fifty cent," replied the Princess.

Nancy had just eight cents at home. Flora had nothing at all. Her father sent her money every month, and the last instalment was all spent. Neither of them could buy the basket, and fifty cents sounded enormous, but their faces were quite dignified and immovable. It might have been the echo of their strange surroundings, but they acted as if they had Indian blood themselves.

They turned about and went out of the tent; they crossed the old road and climbed the stone-wall. Flora spoke as she picked her way across the meadow. "Guess I'll buy that basket when my money comes next week," said she.

Nancy said nothing; she looked gloomy. She stepped in an oozy place and wet one foot, but she did not mind it. She thought of her eight cents, and did an example in mental arithmetic. "Eight from fifty leaves forty-two," she calculated. For the first time she was envious of

Flora. Everybody finds some object to grudge to another. Nancy had found hers—the sweet-grass basket. If she had expressed her feelings, she would have said, "Must she have all those pretty dresses and hats and the sweet-grass basket, too?"

The girls went home silently; they were never great talkers. Flora sat down in the sitting-room with her aunt; Nancy went up-stairs to the chamber where she slept with Flora, and got her little purse out of the corner of her bureau drawer. She counted the eight cents, and puzzled over the problem how to increase it to fifty. She puzzled over it all the rest of that day until she went to sleep at nine o'clock. The next day was Sunday; she puzzled over it as she sat in the pew in church, but she could not arrive at any solution.

However, the next morning she had an inspiration. Her mother sent her over to Aunt Lucretia's on an errand. Flora was not allowed to go; it was a very hot morning, and she was rather delicate. Nancy on her way to Aunt Lucretia's thought of a way to swell eight cents to fifty. She trudged down the sunny road in a cloud of dust, her face was scarlet with the heat, but she ignored all little discomforts.

Aunt Lucretia lived in a nice square white

"SHE WAS A REAL INDIAN PRINCESS"

house with a green lattice-work porch over the front door. She was an elderly lady and quite rich. She had a Brussels carpet in the parlor and kept a servant-maid.

Nancy went in the side door, and through the sitting-room into the front entry. The parlor door stood open. Aunt Lucretia and her servant, Henrietta, were in there. Nancy stood looking in.

"Aunt Lucretia," said she.

Aunt Lucretia came forward, with Henrietta following.

"Well, Nancy, what do you want?" said Aunt Lucretia. She was quite a majestic old lady, very tall and large and short-waisted. She wore her gray hair in two puffs each side of her face.

"Mother sent your Stanford paper back," replied Nancy.

"Well, you can lay it on the sitting-room table," said Aunt Lucretia. "Is your mother well this morning?"

"Yes, ma'am."

Nancy laid the Stanford paper on the sitting-room table; then she followed on into the kitchen after Aunt Lucretia and Henrietta.

"Is there anything else you want, Nancy?" asked Aunt Lucretia.

"I wanted to know if—I didn't know but—

you'd like to have me pick some blackberries for you, Aunt Lucretia."

"Blackberries?"

"Yes, ma'am."

Aunt Lucretia stared reflectively at Nancy. "Do you suppose your mother would be willing? The sun's pretty hot."

"Yes, ma'am. I know she wouldn't care."

"Well, I do want two quarts of blackberries dreadfully, and there 'ain't a boy been along. I'm going to have the minister and his wife to tea to-night, and I want to have blackberry short-cake. Do you suppose you could pick me two quarts before four o'clock this afternoon?"

"Yes, ma'am. I know where they're real thick."

"Well," said Aunt Lucretia, "you can go home and ask your mother, and if she's willing, you can go and pick them. Mind you keep out of the sun all you can. I'll give you seven cents a quart; that's a cent more than the boys ask."

"Don't you want more'n two quarts, Aunt Lucretia?" asked Nancy, timidly.

"I guess two quarts will be about all you'll want to pick," returned Aunt Lucretia, grimly.

"No, ma'am; it won't."

"Well, we'll see how you hold out. I want

four quarts for jell the last of the week; but you pick two quarts first, and see."

Nancy went home. She ran nearly all the way.

"You go right into the sitting-room, and sit down with the palm-leaf fan, and cool off before you do anything else," said her mother, when she proposed the plan; "you'll have a sun-stroke."

So Nancy had to sit in the dark, cool sitting-room and fan herself for full twenty minutes before she was allowed to put on her old dress and Shaker and start on her berrying excursion. Flora wanted to go, too, but her aunt thought it was too hot; she was apt to have headaches. She sat on the back door-step shelling pease when Nancy started.

Nancy, bustling off with her two-quart tin pail, glanced back at Flora's little yellow shaven head bending patiently over the pan of pease in the doorway. She felt guilty. Was she not going off with the secret intention of earning money enough to buy that sweet-grass basket before Flora could? Flora would not have her money until Saturday; this was Monday. If she could only earn the forty-two cents in the mean time.

Nancy worked hard that week. Her hands and arms got scratched; she had even a scratch across her nose. The blackberry vines seemed almost like tangible foes; but she pushed and tussled with them until she had picked the six quarts.

On Monday Aunt Lucretia had the minister and his wife to tea, and made blackberry short-cake; on Friday she made blackberry jelly. All Nancy's part of the contract was promptly fulfilled, but Aunt Lucretia's was not. She had not a cent of change in her purse when Nancy brought in the last instalment of berries.

"You'll have to wait two or three days until I can get this bill changed," said she. "You've been real smart about picking 'em. You've picked 'em clean, too. Here's a piece of sweet-cake for you."

Nancy went home in the hot sun. Her red, scratched face looked gloomy and discouraged in the depths of the Shaker bonnet. She nibbled at the sweet-cake as she went along, but she did not care for it. Here it was Friday forenoon, and she had to wait two or three days for her forty-two cents. Flora's money would come, and she would buy the sweet-grass basket. Nancy felt quite desperate. That afternoon she teased her mother to let her go over to Aunt Lucretia's again.

"No; you don't go a step," said her mother. "She's making jell', and you've been over there once to-day. You can sit down with your knitting-work this afternoon, and be contented."

Nancy sat down with her knitting-work, but she was not contented. It seemed to her that she must have those forty-two cents. After tea she begged again for permission to go to Aunt Lucretia's. "It's real nice and cool out now, mother," she pleaded.

"I don't care how cool it is," said her mother, "you can't go. I don't see what has got into you."

But the next morning Nancy was really sent over to Aunt Lucretia's on an errand. She did the errand, then she stood waiting.

"Did your mother want anything else?" asked Aunt Lucretia.

"No, ma'am."

"Well, I guess you had better run home then. It's baking day, and maybe you can help your mother some. You'd ought to help her all you can, you're getting to be a big girl. I used to do a whole week's baking before I was your age."

"Aunt Lucretia!"

"What say?"

"Have you—got that—bill—changed yet?"

"No, I haven't. You mustn't tease. I'm going down to the store in a day or two, and then you can have it."

So Nancy went home again without her forty-two cents. She wept a little on the way. Here it was Saturday, and Flora expecting her money on the noon mail. But it did not come on the noon mail. It did not come until six o'clock at night, and Flora did not think of buying the basket that day.

After tea that night, about half-past seven o'clock, Nancy did something that she had never done before in her life. She went over to her Aunt Lucretia's without permission. Her mother had gone to one of the neighbor's. Flora was in the sitting-room reading a story-book. Nancy stole out of the front door, and hurried down the road.

"What are you over here again for, child?" Aunt Lucretia cried when she went in.

Aunt Lucretia and Henrietta were in the kitchen, sticking papers over the jelly tumblers.

Nancy hesitated, and blushed.

"What is it?" asked Aunt Lucretia.

"I—didn't know but—what—you might have got—that bill changed."

"Why, I never saw such an acting child! Can't you wait a minute? Henrietta, have you got any change?"

"Yes, ma'am," said Henrietta. And she got her purse, and they counted out forty-two cents. Twenty-two of them were in pennies.

"Now I hope you're satisfied," said Aunt Lucretia, sharply. "Did your mother know you came over here?"

"No, ma'am."

"Well, you're a naughty girl. I'm surprised at you. I sha'n't want to hire you to pick berries again if this is the way you do. Go right home, and mind you tell your mother you've been here."

The forty-two cents, twenty-two of which were pennies, jingled and weighed heavily in Nancy's pocket. She was not happy going home. She had meditated going to the Indian encampment that night to buy the basket, but it looked so dark over the fields that she was afraid to; so she went straight home. Her mother had returned from the neighbor's; there she stood in the front door, watching for her.

"Nancy Mann, I want to know where you've been," she cried out, as soon as Nancy opened the gate.

"Over to—Aunt Lucretia's."

"You went over there, after all the times I told you not to?"

"Yes, ma'am."

"What for?"

"I wanted my—forty-two cents."

"Forty-two cents! What do you suppose your

Aunt Lucretia thinks of you, dunning her up this way? Now you come in and light your candle, and go straight up-stairs to bed."

It was only half-past eight o'clock. Nancy went to bed. Flora sat up and read her story-book, and did not go up-stairs until after nine. Nancy pretended to be asleep when she came in, but she was not. She did not go to sleep for an hour after that. She lay there and cried softly, and planned.

The next morning was very pleasant. It was Sunday, and all the family went to church. After church, Nancy and Flora went to Sunday-school. Sunday-school was out about one o'clock; then they walked homeward together. Nancy lagged behind, and Flora kept waiting for her.

"Go along; do," said Nancy. "I want to pick these flowers."

Flora wondered innocently what Nancy wanted to pick so many flowers for. The flowers were mostly yarrow and arnica blossoms, and Flora had always regarded them as the very commonest kind of weeds.

They were quite near home, when Nancy climbed swiftly over the stone-wall and lay down behind it. Flora went on without turning her head. Nancy had spoken so shortly to her that her feelings were hurt. When she went into the house her aunt asked where Nancy was.

"She's coming," said Flora. "She stopped to pick flowers."

But it was a half-hour before Nancy came. Running as fast as she could over the meadows, it took some time to reach the Indian encampment and return. When she finally approached the house, her mother stood in the doorway, watching. She did not say a word until she came close to her.

"Where have you been?" she inquired.

Nancy hung her head, and was still. She kept one hand behind her.

"Answer me this minute."

"Down to—the Injuns."

"What for? What are you holding behind you?"

Nancy did not answer.

"Bring your hand round!" commanded her mother.

Nancy slowly swung around the hand holding the sweet-grass basket.

"Did you go down to the Injuns to-day, and spend that money you earned for that basket?" asked her mother.

"Yes, ma'am."

Her mother looked at her. The tears were

streaming over her hot cheeks and her scratched nose; her best hat had slipped back, and the brim was bent; there was a great green stain on the front of her best dress, and a rent on the side.

"I can never get that green off your dress in the world," said her mother. "You'll have to wear it so. Going down to the Injuns to buy baskets on Sunday, in your best dress and hat! And you went so Flora should'nt get it. I can see right through you. Now, Nancy Mann, you just march straight back with that basket. You ain't going to do any trading on the Sabbath day while you belong to me."

"Oh, mother!" sobbed Nancy; but she had to go. Her forlorn little figure disappeared lingeringly between the garden vines and bean poles.

"Hold your dress back," called her mother. "Don't you spoil it any more than you've done already."

To Nancy, looking through a mist of tears, the green-clad bean poles seemed dancing forward and the tomato vines creeping to meet her. Crossing the meadow she wet her feet in her best shoes. But all this was nothing. That stout Indian Princess displayed suddenly a sense of humor and a witty shrewdness which seemed abnormal. Her stolid eyes twinkled under their heavy brows when Nancy explained, tremblingly, how she had brought the basket back; her mother would not let her buy it on Sunday.

"Me no buy basket Sunday," said the Princess, and she looked loftily away from the sweet-grass basket shaking in Nancy's shaking hand. She was not in the least moved by Nancy's horrified, distressed face. Perhaps something of the ancient cruelty of her race possessed her; perhaps it was only the contagion of Yankee shrewdness. Nancy dared not go home with the basket; she went home without it or her fifty cents.

All that afternoon Nancy stayed up in her chamber and wept, while her best dress was soaking to remove the green stain, if it was Sunday. She felt as if her heart were broken. She had lost her self-respect, the sweet-grass basket, and her fifty cents, besides getting a great green stain on her best dress. Flora tried to comfort her.

"Don't cry," said she. "It's too bad! The Princess is real mean." And then Nancy sobbed harder.

When her mother was getting supper, her father followed into the pantry.

"I declare I feel sorry for the child," said he. "She's worked real hard to get that money, and she 'ain't ever had so much as Flora. If it wasn't Sunday I'd go down there this minute, and get back the money or the basket from those Injuns."

"You'd look pretty going, and you a deacon of the church, after the way the Princess put it," returned Nancy's mother. "I'm sorry enough for Nancy, but she ought to have a little lesson. You can go over there to-morrow morning and get the basket back."

There was a beautiful custard pudding for supper, but Nancy did not want any.

"Sit up and eat your supper," said her mother. "Your father's going down to the Injuns in the morning, and see what he can do about it."

However, Nancy still did not care for the custard pudding; everything tasted of tears.

The next morning, before Nancy's father had a chance to go to the Indians, the Princess herself came to the back door. Whether she came from honesty or policy nobody could tell; but she came, and she brought the sweet-grass basket. She rapped on the door, and Nancy opened it. The Princess extended the basket without a word. Nancy wiped her hands, which were damp from washing the breakfast dishes, on her apron, then she took the basket. Then the Princess struck off across the garden.

Nancy carried the basket into the kitchen. She had a shamefaced and resolute expression. Flora was in there, and her father and mother.

She went straight to Flora, and held out the basket. Flora drew back, and looked at her.

"Take it," said Nancy. "It's for you."

Flora looked at her aunt.

"Take it, if she wants you to," said Mrs. Mann.

Flora took it. "Thank you," said she. She went soberly out of the room with the basket. Nancy returned to her dish-washing at the sink, her father stared out of the window, her mother came and shoved her aside, and took the dish-cloth out of her hands.

"There, I'll wash this heavy spider," said she. "You can go and put on your other dress. I want you to go down to the store for me, and I'm going to let you buy a couple of yards of that pretty pink calico for a new apron."

Nancy had admired that pink calico. As she went out of the kitchen her father caught her by the shoulders and gave her a little shake; then he patted her head.

"Don't run too fast, and get all tired out," said he.

Nancy put on her buff calico, and went to the store. It was an errand to take about an hour. She had been gone about a half-hour when the Indian Princess again came through the bean poles and tomato vines. This time she was all strung about with baskets. She stood at the kitchen door, and parleyed with Mrs. Mann and Flora. When she went away she had a fifty-cent piece in one brown fist, and she was eating a molasses cooky.

Nancy came home with the pink calico, and half a pound of cream of tartar; her mother and Flora were in the sitting-room, and they laughed when she entered.

Nancy looked soberly at them. "Here's the calico, and the cream tartar," said she.

"See what Flora has got for you," said her mother.

Nancy stared around. There on the table stood two sweet-grass baskets exactly alike.

"The Princess came again, and she had another basket. I got it for you," said Flora.

"Thank you," said Nancy, in a sober voice, but the dark depths of the Shaker bonnet seemed fairly illumined with smiles.

MEHITABLE LAMB

Hannah Maria Green sat on the north door-step, and sewed over and over a seam in a sheet. She had just gotten into her teens, and she was tall for her age, although very slim. She wore a low-necked, and short-sleeved, brown delaine dress. That style of dress was not becoming, but it was the fashion that summer. Her neck was very thin, and her collar-bones showed. Her arms were very long and small and knobby. Hannah Maria's brown hair was parted from her forehead to the back of her neck, braided in two tight braids, crossed in a flat mass at the back of her head, and surmounted by a large green-ribbon bow. Hannah Maria kept patting the bow to be sure it was on.

It was very cool there on the north door-step. Before it lay the wide north yard full of tall waving grass, with some little cinnamon rose-bushes sunken in it. Hardly anybody used the north door, so there was no path leading to it.

It was nearly four o'clock. Hannah Maria bent her sober freckled face over the sheet, and sewed and sewed. Her mother had gone to the next town to do some shopping, and bidden her to finish the seam before she returned. Hannah Maria was naturally obedient; moreover, her mother was a decided woman, so she had been very diligent; in fact the seam was nearly sewed.

It was very still—that is, there were only the sounds that seem to make a part of stillness. The birds twittered, the locusts shrilled, and the tall clock in the entry ticked. Hannah Maria was not afraid, but she was lonesome. Once in a while she looked around and sighed. She placed a pin a little way in advance on the seam, and made up her mind that when she had sewed to that place she would go into the house and get a slice of cake. Her mother had told her that she might cut a slice from the one-egg cake which had been made that morning. But before she had sewed to the pin, little Mehitable Lamb came down the road. She was in reality some years younger than Hannah Maria, but not so much younger as Hannah Maria considered her. The girl on the door-step surveyed the one approaching down the road with a friendly and patronizing air.

"Holloa!" she sang out, when Mehitable was within hailing distance.

"Holloa!" answered back Mehitable's little, sweet, deferential voice.

She came straight on, left the road, and struck across the grassy north yard to Hannah Maria's door-step. She was a round, fair little girl; her auburn hair was curled in a row of neat, smooth "water curls" around her head. She wore a straw hat with a blue ribbon, and a blue-and-white checked gingham dress; she also wore white stockings and patent leather "ankle-ties." Her dress was low-necked and short-sleeved, like Hannah Maria's, but her neck and arms were very fair and chubby.

Mehitable drew her big china doll in a doll's carriage. Hannah Maria eyed her with seeming disdain and secret longing. She herself had given up playing with dolls, her mother thought her too big; but they had still a fascination for her, and the old love had not quite died out of her breast.

"Mother said I might come over and stay an hour and a half," said Mehitable.

Hannah Maria smiled hospitably. "I'm keepin' house," said she. "Mother's gone to Lawrence."

Mehitable took her doll out of the carriage

with a motherly air, and sat down on the doorstep with it in her lap.

"How much longer you goin' to play with dolls?" inquired Hannah Maria.

"I don't know," replied Mehitable, with a little shamed droop of her eyelids.

"You can't when you get a little bigger, anyhow. Is that a new dress she's got on?"

"Yes; Aunt Susy made it out of a piece of her blue silk."

"It's handsome, isn't it? Let me take her a minute." Hannah Maria took the doll and cuddled it up against her shoulder as she had used to do with her own. She examined the blue silk dress. "My doll had a real handsome plaid silk one," said she, and she spoke as if the doll were dead. She sighed.

"Have you given her away?" inquired Mehitable, in a solemn tone.

"No; she's packed away. I'm too old to play with her, you know. Mother said I had other things to 'tend to. Dolls are well 'nough for little girls like you. Here, you'd better take her; I've got to finish my sewin'."

Hannah Maria handed back the doll with a resolute air, but she handed her back tenderly; then she sewed until she reached the pin. Mehitable rocked her doll, and watched.

When Hannah Maria reached the pin she jumped up. "I'm comin' back in a minute," said she, and disappeared in the house. Presently Mehitable heard the dishes rattle.

"She's gone after a cooky," she thought. Cookies were her usual luncheon.

But Hannah Maria came back with a long slice of one-egg cake with blueberries in it. She broke it into halves, and gave the larger one to Mehitable. "There," said she, "I'd give you more, but mother didn't tell me I could cut more'n one slice."

Mehitable ate her cake appreciatively; once in a while she slyly fed her doll with a bit.

Hannah Maria took bites of hers between the stitches; she had almost finished the over-and-over seams.

Presently she rose and shook out the sheet with a triumphant air. "There," said she, "it's done."

"Did you sew all that this afternoon?" asked Mehitable, in an awed tone.

"My! yes. It isn't so very much to do."

Hannah Maria laid the sheet down in a heap on the entry floor; then she looked at Mehitable. "Now, I've nothin' more to do," said she. "S'pose we go to walk a little ways?"

"I don't know as my mother'd like to have me do that."

"Oh yes, she would; she won't care. Come along! I'll get my hat."

Hannah Maria dashed over the sheet into the entry and got her hat off the peg; then she and Mehitable started. They strolled up the country road. Mehitable trundled her doll-carriage carefully; once in a while she looked in to see if the doll was all right.

"Isn't that carriage kind of heavy for you to drag all alone?" inquired Hannah Maria.

"No; it isn't very heavy."

"I had just as lief help you drag it as not."

Hannah Maria reached down and took hold by one side of the handle of the doll-carriage, and the two girls trundled it together.

There were no houses for a long way. The road stretched between pasture-lands and apple-orchards. There was one very fine orchard on both sides of the street a quarter of a mile below Hannah Maria's house. The trees were so heavily loaded with green apples that the branches hung low over the stone walls. Now and then there was among them a tree full of ripe yellow apples.

"Don't you like early apples?" asked Hannah Maria.

Mehitable nodded.

"Had any?"

"No."

"They don't grow in your field, do they?"

Mehitable shook her head. "Mother makes pies with our apples, but they're not mellow 'nough to eat now," she replied.

"Well," said Hannah Maria, "we haven't got any. All our apples are baldwins and greenin's. I havn't had an early apple this summer."

The two went on, trundling the doll-carriage. Suddenly Hannah Maria stopped.

"Look here," said she; "my aunt Jenny and my uncle Timothy have got lots of early apples. You just go along this road a little farther, and you get to the road that leads to their house. S'pose we go."

"How far is it?"

"Oh, not very far. Father walks over sometimes."

"I don't believe my mother would like it."

"Oh yes, she would! Come along."

But all Hannah Maria's entreaties could not stir Mehitable Lamb. When they reached the road that led to Uncle Timothy's house she stood still.

"My mother won't like it," said she.

"Yes, she will."

Mehitable stood as if she and the doll-carriage were anchored to the road.

"I think you're real mean, Mehitable Lamb," said Hannah Maria. "You're a terrible 'fraid cat. I'm goin', anyhow, and I won't bring you a single apple; so there!"

"Don't want any," returned Mehitable, with some spirit. She turned the doll-carriage around. Hannah Maria walked up the road a few steps. Suddenly she faced about. Mehitable had already started homeward.

"Mehitable Lamb!" said she.

Mehitable looked around.

"I s'pose you'll go right straight home and tell my mother just as quick as you can get there."

Mehitable said nothing.

"You'll be an awful telltale if you do."

"Sha'n't tell," said Mehitable, in a sulky voice.

"Will you promise—'Honest and true. Black and blue. Lay me down and cut me in two'—that you won't tell?"

Mehitable nodded.

"Say it over then."

Mehitable repeated the formula. It sounded like inaudible gibberish.

"I shall tell her myself when I get home," said Hannah Maria. "I shall be back pretty soon, anyway, but I don't want her sending father after me. You're sure you're not goin' to tell, now, Mehitable Lamb? Say it over again."

Mehitable said it again.

"Well, you'll be an awful telltale if you do tell after that!" said Hannah Maria.

She went on up one road towards her uncle Timothy Dunn's, and Mehitable trundled her doll-carriage homeward down the other. She went straight on past Hannah Maria's house. Hannah Maria's mother, Mrs. Green, had come home. She saw the white horse and buggy out in the south yard. She heard Mrs. Green's voice calling, "Hannah Maria, Hannah Maria!" and she scudded by like a rabbit.

Mehitable's own house was up the hill, not far beyond. She lived there with her mother and grandmother and her two aunts; her father was dead. The smoke was coming out of the kitchen chimney; her aunt Susy was getting supper. Aunt Susy was the younger and prettier of the aunts. Mehitable thought her perfection. She came to the kitchen door when Mehitable entered the yard, and stood there smiling at her.

"Well," said she, "did you have a nice time at Hannah Maria's?"

"Yes, ma'am."

"What makes you look so sober?"

Mehitable said nothing.

"Did you play dolls?"

"Hannah Maria's too big."

"Stuff!" cried Aunt Susy. Then her short-cake was burning, and she had to run in to see to it.

Mehitable took her china doll out of the carriage, set her carefully on the step, and then lugged the carriage laboriously to a corner of the piazza, where she always kept it. It was a very nice large carriage, and rather awkward to be kept in the house. Then she took her doll and went in through the kitchen to the sitting-room. Her mother and grandmother and other aunt were in there, and they were all glad to see her, and inquired if she had had a nice time at Hannah Maria's. But Mehitable was very sober. She did not seem like herself. Her mother asked whether she did not feel well, and, in spite of her saying that she did, would not let her eat any of her aunt Susy's shortcake for supper. She had to eat some stale bread, and shortly after supper she had to go to bed. Her mother went up-stairs with her, and tucked her in.

"She's all tired out," she said to the others, when she came down; it's quite a little walk over to the Greens', and I s'pose she played hard. I don't really like to have her play with a girl so much older as Hannah Maria. She isn't big enough to run and race."

"She didn't seem like herself when she came into the yard," said Aunt Susy.

"I should have given her a good bowl of thoroughwort tea, when she went to bed," said her grandmother.

"The kitchen fire isn't out yet; I can steep some thoroughwort now," said Aunt Susy, and she forthwith started. She brewed a great bowl of thoroughwort tea and carried it up to Mehitable. Mehitable's wistful innocent blue eyes stared up out of the pillows at Aunt Susy and the bowl.

"What is it?" she inquired.

"A bowl of nice hot thoroughwort tea. You sit up and drink it right down, like a good little girl."

"I'm not sick, Aunt Susy," Mehitable pleaded, faintly. She hated thoroughwort tea.

"Well, never mind if you're not. Sit right up. It'll do you good."

Aunt Susy's face was full of loving determination. So Mehitable sat up. She drank the thoroughwort tea with convulsive gulps. Once in a while she paused and rolled her eyes piteously over the edge of the bowl.

"Drink it right down," said Aunt Susy.

And she drank it down. There never was a more obedient little girl than Mehitable Lamb. Then she lay back, and Aunt Susy tucked her up, and went down with the empty bowl.

"Did she drink it all?" inquired her grandmother.

"Every mite."

"Well, she'll be all right in the morning, I guess. There isn't anything better than a bowl of good, hot, thoroughwort tea."

The twilight was deepening. The Lamb family were all in the sitting-room. They had not lighted the lamp, the summer dusk was so pleasant. The windows were open. All at once a dark shadow appeared at one of them. The women started—all but Grandmother Lamb. She was asleep in her chair.

"Who's there?" Aunt Susy asked, in a grave tone.

"Have you seen anything of Hannah Maria?" said a hoarse voice. Then they knew it was Mr. Green.

Mrs. Lamb and the aunts pressed close to the window.

"No, we haven't," replied Mrs. Lamb. "Why, what's the matter?"

"We can't find her anywheres. Mother went over to Lawrence this afternoon, and I was down in the east field hayin'. Mother, she got home first, and Hannah Maria wasn't anywhere about the house, an' she'd kind of an idea she'd gone over to the Bennets'; she'd been talkin' about goin' there to get a tidy-pattern of the Bennet girl, so she waited till I got home. I jest put the horse in again, an' drove over there, but she's not been there. I don't know where she is. Mother's most crazy."

"Where is she?" they cried, all altogether.

"Sittin' out in the road, in the buggy."

Mrs. Lamb and the aunts hurried out. They and Mr. Green stood beside the buggy, and Mrs. Green thrust her anxious face out.

"Oh, where do you suppose she is?" she groaned.

"Now, do keep calm, Mrs. Green," said Mrs. Lamb, in an agitated voice. "We've got something to tell you. Mehitable was over there this afternoon."

"Oh, she wasn't, was she?"

"Yes, she was. She went about four o'clock, and she stayed an hour and a half. Hannah Maria was all right then. Now, I tell you what we'll do, Mrs. Green: you just get right out of the buggy, and Mr. Green will hitch the horse, and we'll go in and ask Mehitable just how she left Hannah Maria. Don't you worry. You keep calm, and we'll find her."

Mrs. Green stepped tremblingly from the buggy. She could scarcely stand. Mrs. Lamb took one arm and Aunt Susy the other. Mr. Green hitched the horse, and they all went into the house, and up-stairs to Mehitable's room. Mehitable was not asleep. She stared at them in a frightened way as they all filed into the room. Mrs. Green rushed to the bed.

"Oh, Mehitable," she cried, "when did you last see my Hannah Maria?"

Mehitable looked at her and said nothing.

"Tell Mrs. Green when you last saw Hannah Maria," said Mrs. Lamb.

"I guess 'twas 'bout five o'clock," replied Mehitable, in a quavering voice.

"She got home at half-past five," interposed Mehitable's mother.

"Did she look all right?" asked Mrs. Green.

"Yes, ma'am."

"Nobody came to the house when you were there, did there?" asked Mr. Green.

"No, sir."

Aunt Susy came forward. "Now look here, Mehitable," said she. "Do you know anything about what has become of Hannah Maria? Answer me, yes or no."

Mehitable's eyes were like pale moons; her little face was as white as the pillow.

"Yes, ma'am."

"Well, what has become of her?"

Mehitable was silent.

"Why, Mehitable Lamb!" repeated Aunt Susy, "tell us this minute what has become of Hannah Maria!"

Mehitable was silent.

"Oh," sobbed Mrs. Green, "you must tell me. Mehitable, you'll tell Hannah Maria's mother what has become of her, won't you?"

Mehitable's mother bent over her and whispered, but Mehitable lay there like a little stone image.

"Oh, do make her tell!" pleaded Mrs. Green.

"Come, now, tell, and I'll buy you a whole pound of candy," said Mr. Green.

"Mehitable, you *must* tell," said Aunt Susy.

Suddenly Mehitable began to cry. She sobbed and sobbed; her little body shook convulsively. They all urged her to tell, but she only shook her head between the sobs.

Grandmother Lamb came into the room. She had awakened from her nap.

"What's the matter?" she inquired. "What ails Mehitable? Is she sick?"

"Hannah Maria is lost, and Mehitable knows what has become of her, and she won't tell," explained Aunt Susy.

"Massy sakes!" Grandmother Lamb went up to the bed. "Tell grandmother," she whispered, "an' she'll give you a pep'mint."

But Mehitable shook her head and sobbed.

They all pleaded and argued and commanded, but they got no reply but that shake of the head and sobs.

"The child will be sick if she keeps on this way," said Grandmother Lamb.

"She deserves to be sick!" said Hannah Maria's mother, in a desperate voice; and Mehitable's mother forgave her.

"We may as well go down," said Mr. Green, with a groan. "I can't waste any more time here; I've got to do something."

"Oh, here 'tis night coming on, and my poor child lost!" wailed Hannah Maria's mother.

Mehitable sobbed so that it was pitiful in spite of her obstinacy.

"If that child don't have somethin' to take, she'll be sick," said her grandmother. "I dunno as there's any need of her bein' sick if Hannah Maria *is* lost." And she forthwith went stiffly down-stairs. The rest followed—all except Mrs. Lamb. She lingered to plead longer with Mehitable.

"You're mother's own little girl," said she, "and nobody shall scold you whatever happens. Now, tell mother what has become of Hannah Maria."

But it was of no use. Finally, Mrs. Lamb

tucked the clothes over Mehitable with a jerk, and went down-stairs herself. They were having a consultation there in the sitting-room. It was decided that Mr. Green should drive to Mr. Pitkin's, about a quarter of a mile away, and see if they knew anything of Hannah Maria, and get Mr. Pitkin to aid in the search.

"I wouldn't go over to Timothy's to-night, if I were you," said Mrs. Green. "Jenny's dreadful nervous, and it would use her all up; she thought so much of Hannah Maria."

Mrs. Green's voice broke with a sob.

"No, I'm not going there," returned Mr. Green. "It isn't any use. It isn't likely they know anything about her. It's a good five mile off."

Mr. Green got into his buggy and drove away. Mrs. Green went home, and Aunt Susy and the other aunt with her. Nobody slept in the Lamb or the Green house that night, except Grandmother Lamb. She dozed in her chair, although they could not induce her to go to bed. But first she started the kitchen fire, and made another bowl of thoroughwort tea for Mehitable.

"She'll be sick jest as sure as the world, if she doesn't drink it," said she. And Mehitable lifted her swollen, teary face from the pillow and drank it. "She don't know any more where that Green girl has gone to than I do," said Grandmother

Lamb, when she went down with the bowl. "There isn't any use in pesterin' the child so."

Mrs. Lamb watched for Mr. Green to return from Mr. Pitkin's, and ran out to the road. He had with him Mr. Pitkin's hired man and eldest boy.

"Pitkin's harnessed up and gone the other way, over to the village, and we're goin' to look round the place thorough, an'—look in the well," he said, in a husky voice.

"If she would only tell," groaned Mrs. Lamb. "I've done all I can. I can't *make* her speak."

Mr. Green groaned in response, and drove on. Mrs. Lamb went in, and stood at her sitting-room window and watched the lights over at the Green house. They flitted from one room to another all night. At dawn Aunt Susy ran over with her shawl over her head. She was wan and hollow-eyed.

"They haven't found a sign of her," said she. "They've looked everywhere. The Pitkin boy's been down the well. Mr. Pitkin has just come over from the village, and a lot of men are going out to hunt for her as soon as it's light. If Mehitable only would tell!"

"I can't make her," said Mrs. Lamb, despairingly.

"I know what I think you'd ought to do," said Aunt Susy, in a desperate voice.

"What?"

"*Whip her.*"

"Oh, Susy, I can't! I never whipped her in my life."

"Well, I don't care. I should." Aunt Susy had the tragic and resolute expression of an inquisitor. She might have been proposing the rack. "I think it is your duty," she added.

Mrs. Lamb sank into the rocking-chair and wept; but within an hour's time Mehitable stood shivering and sobbing in her night-gown, and held out her pretty little hands while her mother switched them with a small stick. Aunt Susy was crying down in the sitting-room. "Did she tell?" she inquired, when her sister, quite pale and trembling, came in with the stick.

"No," replied Mrs. Lamb. "I never will whip that dear child again, come what will." And she broke the stick in two and threw it out of the window.

As the day advanced teams began to pass the house. Now and then one heard a signal horn. The search for Hannah Maria was being organized. Mrs. Lamb and the aunts cooked a hot breakfast, and carried it over to Mr. and Mrs. Green. They felt as if they must do something to prove their regret and sympathy. Mehitable was up and dressed, but her poor little auburn locks were not curled, and the pink roundness seemed gone from her face. She sat quietly in her little chair in the sitting-room and held her doll. Her mother had punished her very tenderly, but there were some red marks on her little hands. She had not eaten any breakfast, but her grandmother had kindly made her some thoroughwort tea. The bitterness of life seemed actually tasted to poor little Mehitable Lamb.

It was about nine o'clock, and Mrs. Lamb and the aunts had just carried the hot breakfast over to the Green's, and were arranging it on the table, when another team drove into the yard. It was a white horse and a covered wagon. On the front seat sat Hannah Maria's aunt, Jenny Dunn, and a young lady, one of Hannah Maria's cousins. Mrs. Green ran to the door. "Oh, Jenny, *have* you heard?" she gasped. Then she screamed, for Hannah Maria was peeking out of the rear of the covered wagon. She was in there with another young lady cousin, and a great basket of yellow apples.

"Hannah Maria Green, where *have* you been?" cried her mother.

"Why, what do you think! That child walked 'way over to our house last night," Aunt Jenny said, volubly; "and Timothy was gone with the horse, and there wasn't anything to do but to keep her. I knew you wouldn't be worried about her, for she said the little Lamb girl knew where she'd gone, and—"

Mrs. Green jerked the wagon door open and pulled Hannah Maria out. "Go right into the house!" she said, in a stern voice. "Here she wouldn't tell where you'd gone. And the whole town hunting! Go in."

Hannah Maria's face changed from uneasy and deprecating smiles to the certainty of grief. "Oh, I made her promise not to tell, but I s'posed she would," she sobbed. "I didn't know 'twas going to be so far. Oh, mother, I'm sorry!"

"Go right in," said her mother.

And Hannah Maria went in. Aunt Susy and Mrs. Lamb pushed past her as she entered. They were flying home to make amends to Mehitable, with kind words and kisses, and to take away the taste of the thoronghwort tea with sponge-cake and some of the best strawberry jam.

Later in the forenoon Mehitable, with the row of smooth water-curls round her head, dressed in her clean pink calico, sat on the door-step with her doll. Her face was as smiling as the china one. Hannah Maria came slowly into the yard. She carried a basket of early apples. Her eyes were red. "Here are some apples for you," she said. "And I'm sorry I made you so much trouble. I'm not going to eat any."

"Thank you," said Mehitable. "Did your mother scold?" she inquired, timidly.

"She did first. I'm dreadful sorry. I won't ever do so again. I—kind of thought you'd tell."

"I'm not a telltale," said Mehitable.

"No, you're not," said Hannah Maria.

THE END.

www.ingramcontent.com/pod-product-compliance
Lightning Source LLC
Chambersburg PA
CBHW031350230426
43670CB00006B/497